1 and 2
PETER

1 and 2
PETER

ROBERT K. McIVER

Pacific Press®
Publishing Association
Nampa, Idaho | Oshawa, Ontario, Canada
www.pacificpress.com

The author assumes full responsibility for the accuracy of all facts and quotations as cited in this book.

You can obtain additional copies of this book by calling toll-free 1-800-765-6955 or by visiting http://www.adventistbookcenter.com.

Library of Congress Cataloging-in-Publication Data
Names: McIver, Robert K. (Robert Kerry), 1953- author.
Title: 1 and 2 Peter / Robert K. McIver.
Other titles: First and second Peter
Description: Nampa, Idaho : Pacific Press Publishing Association, 2016.
Identifiers: LCCN 2016029017 | ISBN 9780816361830 (pbk.)
Subjects: LCSH: Bible. Peter--Criticism, interpretation, etc.
Classification: LCC BS2795.52 .M35 2016 | DDC 227/.9207--dc23 LC record available at https://lccn.loc.gov/2016029017

September 2016

Dedication

For the girls who light up my life:

Susan, Althea and Skye

Acknowledgments

I have many to thank in helping me with various stages of the process by which this book came into being. I thank Roger Govender for recommending me as a potential contributor of a Sabbath School study guide, Clifford Goldstein for extending the invitation to write and his fine editorial work on the *Adult Sabbath School Study Guide*, to those from the different regions of the world church who reviewed the lessons, and for Scott Cady and Pacific Press for asking me to write the companion book. I thank Avondale College of Higher Education for support in my research for writing the quarterly and companion book, particularly for their underwriting of an all-too-brief time at Tyndale House in Cambridge, where I was able to take advantage of their very high quality library. I thank my wife, Susan, for her continued patience and support as this book was written to a very tight deadline. I also would like to thank Jon Paulien of Loma Linda University, California, and Cedric Vine of Andrews University, Michigan, for providing academic referees' reports for this book.

Contents

Preface

This book starts with a careful examination of the text of 1 and 2 Peter and then teases out the implications that the words of Peter have for the everyday life of a Christian. It has many of the characteristics of a commentary. For example, it considers the historical, social, and literary background of the passages under consideration, and it comments on the meaning of many of the key words and other features of the Greek text of the epistles. From time to time it does what Peter himself does in his letters by considering the practical application of the theology expressed to the everyday life of Christians.

While it stands alone in its own right, this book is also written to be a companion volume to the *Adult Sabbath School Study Guide* that will be used in the second quarter of 2017 by the majority of the more than 78,000 Seventh-day Adventist churches scattered across the globe.* It has been interesting for me to discover how the knowledge that a particular passage of Scripture is being studied in a local church environment has enriched the

---

* The most recent official statistics from the church available at the time of writing, the *2015 Annual Statistical Report: 151st Report of the General Conference of Seventh-day Adventists for 2013 and 2014* (p. 29), reveal that in December 2013, the church acknowledged 76,364 official Seventh-day Adventist churches globally, a number that had increased to 78,810 by the end of 2014.

range of materials that I felt belonged in this book.

I had always wanted to write a Sabbath School study guide, so I felt very privileged when approached to do so by Clifford Goldstein in 2011 to write on 1 and 2 Peter. When it came time to write the study guide, I discovered it a challenge, albeit a pleasurable one, to write something of significance given the constraints of the small word budget for the comment for each day's "study" that also had to include questions for meditation and discussion, quotations from authors, and the like. Although there is still a tight word budget for this book, I have enjoyed the extra freedom it has provided for me to interact more closely with the text of 1 and 2 Peter than was possible in the study guide.

Robert K. McIver
Cooranbong, Australia
March 31, 2016

Introduction

I recently took the opportunity to listen in on some sessions on 1 and 2 Peter while attending the Society of Biblical Literature meetings. One evening, I was invited to join a friend and one of the presenters for a meal. During the meal I fell into conversation with the scholar, who specialized in 1 and 2 Peter, and asked him what had led him to choose this particular part of the New Testament to study. He explained that as a PhD student, he worked with a supervisor who was a very famous and widely published professor with a reputation of being very involved with his student's PhD dissertations. He then explained that when he was trying to settle on the research topic, he took one suggestion after another to his supervisor, who would then say, "Yes, I have written something on that topic and can help you a great deal with it. First you will . . ." At which point my friend would go away and think of a new topic, whereupon the supervisor would respond, "Yes, I have written something on that topic and can help you a great deal with it. First you will . . ." Finally, my friend suggested a topic in 1 and 2 Peter, and the professor said, "Yes . . . you know . . . I don't know much about 1 and 2 Peter at all." And so my friend began a career as a specialist in 1 and 2 Peter. A good choice, as it turns out, because he has been able to make significant contributions to our understanding of these books.

I think this is a wonderful story which beautifully illustrates the relative attention given to 1 and 2 Peter in the academic world. While there are significant commentaries and articles written on these two letters, much less is written on 1 and 2 Peter compared to the amount written about the letters of Paul, the four Gospels, and the Apocalypse of John. In some respects, the relative neglect of 1 and 2 Peter can be understood. The Gospels record the deeds and sayings of the Founder of Christianity. The letters of Paul carry within them profound ideas that have shaped much of Christian theology, and they have played a significant role in the extraordinary upheaval associated with the emergence of Protestantism. First and 2 Peter, on the other hand, are quite small letters tucked away toward the back of the New Testament, and written to address situations that can seem alien to the modern reader.

Yet, as will emerge in the following chapters, there is much to commend 1 and 2 Peter to our attention. Though the letters were written to people very different in culture and circumstances than those living today, Peter addresses their concerns with carefully reasoned answers, rich in theology and practical advice. The resultant letters have many interesting features. We discover something of the stressful circumstances that the early Christian believers in Asia Minor were facing and how Peter addresses their real concerns. We find out that there are false teachers troubling these very churches and discover the consequences of their teaching in the lives of those whom they influence. The theology that Peter shares has been formed to meet very practical needs. Because of that, they have a relevance to contemporary believers that is quite remarkable.

The following chapters explore the concerns that Peter had regarding the Christian communities he addressed and his response to their circumstances. The first chapter looks at Peter himself to discover the stature of the one from whom these letters originated. The next eleven chapters deal with the leading ideas covered in the two letters, more or less in the order in which they are found in the letters. The final chapter looks at some of the larger themes that emerged as we studied the details of the letters.

Meet the Author: Peter

The letters of Peter were written by a prominent disciple of Jesus[1] who became a significant leader in early Christianity. We probably know more about Peter than any of the other disciples— both positive and negative. It is not surprising that we know a lot of good things about such a very prominent leader among the earliest followers of Jesus. After all, positive stories are usually circulated about the prominent leaders of groups. So when you think about it, it is remarkable how many *negative* things we know about Peter given his leadership role.

As we review some of the major incidents in the New Testament that involve Peter to better understand his letters, we will discover anew that Peter was a person who made mistakes and was forgiven by his Lord. Peter, then, is somebody not unlike us when it comes to mistakes, and he can show us what it really means to be a true follower of Jesus in an imperfect world.

"Depart from me; for I am a sinful man" (Luke 5:1-11)

When we first meet Peter in the Gospels, he is working as a fisherman in the northern parts of the lake of Gennaserat (Luke 5:1; this lake is also known as the Sea of Galilee, e.g., Matthew 4:18). He worked with his brother, Andrew (Matthew 4:18), in partnership with James and John, the sons of Zebedee (Luke 5:10).

1 and 2 Peter

Peter was originally from Bethsaida, a small fishing village on the northern shores of Lake Gennaserat (John 1:44). By the time Jesus moved to Capernaum at the beginning of His public ministry (Matthew 4:12, 13; Luke 4:31), Peter was apparently spending much of his time there (e.g., Matthew 17:24; the village where his mother-in-law lived, Luke 4:31, 38, 39). Like Bethsaida, Capernaum was a small fishing village. Its mainly one-story, stone-walled houses were spread along the lakeshore, where there was a seawall and paved promenade. There were several piers against which boats could be moored. In the time of Jesus there were between eight hundred and fifteen hundred inhabitants.[2]

Luke 5:1–11 records the dramatic occurrences surrounding the moment Peter accepted Jesus' call to become His disciple. Along the lakeshore between Capernaum and Bethsaida there are a number of inlets that are shaped like natural amphitheaters, and apparently Peter and the others had chosen such an inlet to bring their boats ashore after an unsuccessful night's fishing. A large crowd had gathered around Jesus, and He asked Peter to move the boat a little way from the shore so that He could speak to the crowds more easily. The natural shape of the shoreline would enable His voice to carry.

After Jesus finished speaking, He asked Peter to go out again into deep water to lower the nets. Peter explained that they had been doing this all night without result, but that because Jesus said to do so, they would do it. They caught so many fish they needed help to bring them to shore. Peter's response was to fall down at Jesus' knees and say, "Depart from me; for I am a sinful man, O Lord" (verse 8, KJV). Jesus responded by reassuring Peter, "Do not be afraid; from now on you will be catching people" (verse 10, NRSV). As a result of hearing Jesus' teaching, seeing the miracle of the fish, and hearing the words, "Follow me, and I will make you fishers of men" (Matthew 4:19, KJV), Peter, Andrew, James, and John left everything behind and followed Jesus—including their equipment and the miraculous catch of fish. If nothing else, this shows the life-changing effect that Jesus had on those with whom He came in contact.

Peter went on to become one of Jesus' closest disciples. For example, only Peter, James, and John were present when Jesus brought a dead girl back to life (Luke 8:49–59), only they accompanied Jesus to the Mount of Transfiguration (Luke 9:28–36), and they went farther than the other disciples with Him into the Garden of Gethsemane the night He was betrayed (Mark 14:32, 33). Peter usually acted as a spokesperson for the disciples, and in Matthew, the list of the twelve disciples is headed by "first Simon, who is called Peter" (Matthew 10:2).

Confessing Jesus as the Christ (Matthew 16:13-23)

Matthew 16:13–23, Mark 8:27–30, and Luke 9:18–20 all recount the incident when Jesus asked "Who do the crowds say that I am?" The disciples answered that He was called John the Baptist or Elijah. When Jesus asked, "But who do you say that I am?" Peter answered, "The Christ [Messiah] of God." This is where the story finishes in both Mark and Luke. Matthew seems to have a special interest in Peter, who includes several sayings and even whole stories about Peter that are only found in his Gospel. One place where he does this is Matthew 16:17–23, which provides more details about what happened, including the very famous response that Jesus made to Peter's words, "You are Peter [Greek *Petros*], and on this rock [Greek *petra*] I will build my church" (Matthew 16:18, NRSV). Jesus even goes on to say to Peter, "I will give you the keys of the kingdom of heaven, and whatever you bind on earth will have been bound in heaven, and whatever you loose on earth will have been loosed in heaven."[3]

These words were used by the medieval papacy to assert their right to lock the kingdom of heaven against those whom they excommunicated. Luther took exception to this interpretation, and debate has raged as to the meaning of these words to this day. Some scholars wish to see Peter as the chief rabbi and understand these words as giving him authority to interpret the law for early Christianity. Others point out that what is said of Peter here is also said of the whole Christian community in Matthew 18:18 and conclude that Peter is portrayed in the Gospel of Matthew as nothing more than an ideal disciple.[4] It will not be possible to explore all the arguments here,[5] but three observations may be made:

1. Jesus' approval of Peter is bound up with his confession that Jesus is the Messiah. But Peter and Jesus have different conceptions of the Messiah. For Jesus, the Messiah will suffer and die (Matthew 16:21), yet Peter would not hear of it (verse 22). Jesus was so concerned about this response He said to Peter, "Get behind me, Satan!" (verse 23, NRSV). From this it is clear that Jesus' affirmation of Peter is conditional on him understanding that Jesus is the Messiah who suffers.

2. When Peter (and the community) bind or loose on earth, they are only making real something that has already happened in heaven (notice the tense, "will have bound . . . will have loosed"). It is not Peter who is shutting up heaven, but Peter reflecting on earth a decision that has already been made in heaven.

3. Peter does have the authority of a leader in the early church, but this authority flows from the fact that he is a follower of Jesus. Peter is, in this way, the ideal disciple, the spokesman of the disciples, and an example to all Christians, at least as long as he is following his Lord.

Walking on water (Matthew 14:22-33)

The story of Jesus walking on the water to join His disciples in their boat while caught in a storm is recounted in three of the four Gospels (Matthew 14:22–33; Mark 6:45–52; John 6:15–21). Only Matthew records Peter's request to Jesus that he come join Him on the water (Matthew 14:28–33). Jesus replied, "Come," and Peter stepped out onto the water and started walking toward Jesus. "But when he noticed the strong wind, he became frightened, and beginning to sink, he cried out, 'Lord, save me!' " (Matthew 14:30, NRSV). Jesus rescues Peter, and on their joining the rest of the disciples in the boat, the storm immediately ceased, whereupon the disciples worshiped Jesus, saying, "Truly you are the Son of God" (verse 33, NRSV).

In this story Peter is able to perform an amazing feat—walking on water. But he can do this only while his eyes are fixed on Jesus. As soon as his attention wanders from Jesus, he begins to sink. As Ellen G. White says, "When trouble comes upon us, how often we are like Peter! We look upon the waves, instead of keeping our eyes fixed upon the Saviour."[6]

Denying his Lord (Luke 22:31-33; 22:54-62)

All four Gospels record that Peter denied Jesus. The story they recount is this: Following the arrest of Jesus in the Garden of Gethsemane, all but two of the disciples fled. A combination of loyalty and courage led Peter and John to separately follow Jesus (John 18:15, 16). Who knows what was going through Peter's head? But given his impetuosity, he may have been looking for an opportunity to rescue Jesus, or at least find out what was happening to Him. Well aware of the danger, he decided to keep a low profile, and when accused of being a follower of Jesus, he denied it on three separate occasions (Luke 22:54–62). At that moment Jesus turned and looked a Peter, and Peter remembered what Jesus had told him earlier, " 'Before the cock crows today, you will deny me three times.' And he went out and wept bitterly" (verses 61, 62, NRSV).

Two of the disciples denied Jesus that night—Judas Iscariot and Peter. Judas tried to undo the evil he had done, and when he could not, he committed suicide (Matthew 27:3–10). Peter was sorry for what he had done, but he clung to Jesus' assurance that Jesus Himself had prayed for him. Peter was able to repent and go on to meet the risen Jesus. During that meeting Jesus gave Peter opportunity to express his love three times (John 21:15–23).[7]

Early church leader (Acts 2-11; Galatians 1:18, 19; 2:9, 11-14)

Peter's prominent role in the early Christian church is revealed by how frequently his name appears in the early chapters of Acts. After the Holy Spirit descended on the disciples, it was Peter who gave the first public speech/sermon about Jesus (Acts 2:1–36, esp. verse 14). As a result of this speech, about three thousand believers were "added" to the number who followed Jesus (verse 41). It was Peter (and John) who healed the crippled beggar (Acts 3:1–8), and again, Peter preached publically in the temple (verses 11–16).

Later, Peter and John spoke to the rulers, elders, and scribes to defend their actions (Acts 4:1–22). It was Peter who spoke up from prison that they "must obey God rather than any human authority" (Acts 5:29, NRSV). It was Peter who was there when the first Gentiles joined the followers of Jesus (Acts 10:1–48) and who reported back to the rest of the believers that since Gentiles had received the Holy Spirit they should be considered part of the group (Acts 11:1–18). Finally, Paul speaks of Peter when describing his visit to Jerusalem, where he met with James and Cephas (i.e., Peter) and John, "who were acknowledged pillars" (Galatians 2:9).

How knowing about the author helps in understanding 1 and 2 Peter

As we consider 1 and 2 Peter in the following chapters, we will have occasion to look back on what we know about Peter many times. For example:

1. Peter's status as a prominent disciple of Jesus and early leader of Christianity gives him the authority to write a letter to the Christian communities scattered across Asia Minor. His position also makes it more likely that his letters would be attended to with great interest and is no doubt the reason they were preserved and included in the works of the New Testament.

2. Peter's background as a Galilean fisherman means we know his primary language (Aramaic) and can deduce much about his education. Like others of his time and place, he would have received some formal instruction at the local synagogue and learned to read from the Hebrew Scriptures.[8] It is highly unlikely that Peter had a formal introduction to Greek as a youth. While it is possible that Peter was one of those rare individuals who quickly learns a language well enough to pass as a local, it is more likely that his Greek was of a very rough-and-ready nature. Given the very high quality of the Greek in both 1 and 2 Peter, I think it very probable that Peter relied very heavily on his secretaries in polishing his letters (see comments on Silvanus in chapter 2 and in the first footnote of this chapter).

3. In 2 Peter 1:16–18, Peter emphasizes the fact that he was an eyewitness of the majesty of Jesus. In fact, Peter and the other

disciples were in the front row, as it were, when Jesus was teaching, healing, and talking with others. Peter says many things about Jesus in his letters; and when Peter talks about Jesus, he speaks with the authority of one who knows Him well.

4. When Peter emphasizes the centrality of forgiveness and love in the life of the Christian, we know that he does so because he has experienced the love and forgiveness of Jesus. Peter deserves a good hearing, because when he speaks of the essentials of Christianity, he is speaking of what he knows personally!

Knowing Peter's story provides a very helpful background that gives his writing added credibility and brings understanding to many crucial points.

---

1. It would be more accurate to say that the letters were "dictated" by Peter, as it was common in the first century to use an amanuensis (secretary) when composing letters. Even Paul did this. I often ask my classes, "Who wrote Romans?" Their answer, "Paul," is technically incorrect, because as Romans 16:22 says, "I Tertius, the writer of this letter, greet you in the Lord." Strictly, then, Tertius "wrote" the letter to the Romans; Paul dictated it to him. Peter would have done the same if he was the author of 1 and 2 Peter. It must be admitted that academics debate whether or not Peter was actually involved in the writing of 1 and 2 Peter, but most conservative scholars consider that Peter the apostle is responsible for 1 Peter. Peter does say, though, in 1 Peter 5:12 that he wrote the letter with the help of Silvanus (or Silas), who was at the very least an amanuensis, but may have given more substantial help in improving the language of the letter. While there are some exceptions (e.g., N. T. Wright, *1 & 2 Peter and Jude* [Downers Grove, IL: IVP Connect, 2012], 5; Richard Bauckham, *Jude–2 Peter*, Word Biblical Commentary, rev. ed. [Grand Rapids, MI: Zondervan, 2014], 143–151), many, if not most, conservative scholars would agree with me that 2 Peter also comes from Peter the apostle (e.g., Gene L. Green, *Jude & 2 Peter*, Baker Exegetical Commentary on the New Testament [Grand Rapids, MI: Baker Academic, 2008], 139–150; F. D. Nichol, ed., *The Seventh-day Adventist Bible Commentary*, rev. ed. [Washington, DC: Review and Herald®, 1980], 5:185, 186; 7:593). The Greek of both letters is described as very good Greek by ancient and modern readers alike (e.g., it is composed using very long and complex sentences), although the Greek of 2 Peter is slightly different than that of 1 Peter. The thoughts are those of Peter, but how much of the style of the letter should be attributed to him and how much to his amanuensis/helpers is hard to say. We know Peter was a Galilean fisherman who most likely grew up speaking Aramaic, so Greek would be a second language to him, and his Greek may have been

poor. Yet he is comfortable traveling through the Greek and Latin-speaking parts of the Roman Empire and may have had a natural ear for languages—some people do. Or he may have done what many leaders today do when they are sending out letters that will be read by many people—work closely with others to improve the quality of the writing expressing his thoughts. *The Seventh-day Adventist Bible Commentary* suggests that the differences in the language between 1 and 2 Peter would most likely be attributed to Peter using a different amanuensis for 2 Peter (*The Seventh-day Adventist Bible Commentary* 5:185, 186; cf. a very similar suggestion made by Michael Green, *The Second Epistle General of Peter and the General Epistle of Jude* [Leicester/Grand Rapids, MI: IVP/Eerdmans, 1987], 15, 16).

2. See discussion of what archaeology has revealed about Capernaum in Robert K. McIver, "Archaeology of Galilee," in Mark Harding and Alana Nobbs, eds., *Content and Setting of the Gospel Tradition* (Grand Rapids, MI: Eerdmans, 2010), 9–12.

3. ". . . will have been bound . . . will have been loosed" is my own translation that matches the underlying Greek tense (a future perfect periphrastic for the technically inclined; see list of periphrastic tenses in Robert K. McIver, *Intermediate New Testament Greek Made Easier* [Cooranbong, NSW, Australia: Barnard, 2015], 128, 129; Daniel B. Wallace, *Greek Grammar Beyond the Basics* [Grand Rapids, MI: Zondervan, 1996], 647–649). The KJV, NKJV, NIV, RSV, and NRSV all translate this as ". . . shall/will be bound . . . shall/will be loosed," which is a translation that poorly represents the tense of the Greek text reporting the words of Jesus.

4. See the arguments for and against these two positions in Jack Dean Kingsbury, "The Figure of Peter in Matthew's Gospel as a Theological Problem," *Journal of Biblical Literature* 98 (1979): 67–83. This is an older article but still one of the clearest explanations of the various options that have been argued for the role of Peter as he is portrayed in the Gospel of Matthew.

5. See Robert K. McIver, *Mainstream or Marginal? The Matthean Community in Early Christianity* (Frankfurt am Main, Germany: Lang, 2012), 117–123, for a more detailed (if somewhat technical because it relies on the Greek of the passage and the Hebrew background of some of the terms) examination of the evidence regarding Peter in the Gospel of Matthew.

6. Ellen G. White, *The Desire of Ages* (Mountain View, CA: Pacific Press®, 1940), 382. In a famous essay, first published in German in 1948, Günther Bornkamm suggests, "Matthew is not only a hander-on of the narrative, but also its oldest exegete [interpretor], and in fact the first to interpret the journey of the disciples with Jesus in the storm as the stilling of the storm with reference to discipleship, and that means with reference to the little ship of the Church." "The Stilling of the Storm in Matthew," in Günther Bornkamm, Gerhard Bath, and Heinz Joachim Held, *Tradition and Interpretation in Matthew* (Philadelphia: Westminster, 1963), 55. This article is included in the collection of Bornkamm's works edited by Werner Zager, *Studien zum Mat-*

thäus-Evangelium (Neukirchen-Vluyn: Neukirchener, 2009), 73–78.

7. There is a subtle interplay in these verses between two Greek words for love that are almost synonymous (*agapaō* and *phileō*). In John 21:15, 16, Jesus twice asks Peter "Do you love (*agapaō*) me?" Peter replies, "I love (*philō*) you." Finally, Jesus asks Peter, "Do you love (*fileis*) me?" (verse 17). Whereupon Peter states again, "I love (*philō*) you." David Shepherd has argued (successfully I think) that the appearance of *agapaō* in Jesus first two questions points back to the discussion of love in John 13 through 17. Particularly such verses as John 15:13, that there is no greater love (*apapēn,* the noun that corresponds to the verb *agapaō*) than that somebody should lay down their life for their friends. See David Shepherd, " 'Do You Love Me?' A Narrative-Critical Reappraisal of ἀγαπάω and φιλέω in John 21:15–17," *Journal of Biblical Literature* 129 (2010): 777–792. It seems that even after the lessons of the crucifixion of Jesus, Peter still had things yet to learn!

8. Birger Gerhardsson, *Memory and Manuscript* (Grand Rapids, MI: Eerdmans, 1998), 85–92; S. Safrai, "Education and the Study of the Torah," in S. Safrai and M. Stern, eds., *The Jewish People in the First Century* (Amsterdam: Van Gorcum, 1976), 2:949. Catherine Hezser suggests, "The Jewish schools to which rabbinic sources refer are likely to have taught reading skills only." *Jewish Literacy in Roman Palestine* (Tübingen, Germany: Mohr Siebeck, 2001), 39.

CHAPTER 2

God, Salvation, and Consequences
1 Peter 1:1-2:3

First Peter begins in the same way as most other ancient letters: it identifies the author and the recipient.[1] It is from "Peter, an apostle of Jesus Christ," and is sent "to the exiles of the Dispersion in Pontus, Galatia, Cappadocia, Asia, and Bithynia" (1 Peter 1:1, NRSV).

Exiles of the Dispersion

Peter writes to the "exiles of the Dispersion." These words reveal much about those to whom he writes. For example, the word translated "Dispersion" is *diasporas* (a form of the word *diaspora*). This word is used twelve times in the Septuagint (the Greek version of the Old Testament) to describe Jews who were scattered among the Gentiles,[2] and is used in this sense in John 7:35. Thus the natural way for Peter's words to be read is to understand that he is sending his letter to Jewish Christians. Peter, after all, "had been entrusted with the gospel for the circumcised [i.e., Jews]," while Paul "had been entrusted with the gospel to the uncircumcised" (Galatians 2:7, NRSV). It would make sense, then, that he should write this letter to those Jews who had become Christians. On the other hand, there is some evidence that the churches to which Peter was writing included some Gentiles in their numbers. For example, 1 Peter 1:18 and

4:3 seem more natural if addressed to Gentiles.

Pontus, Galatia, Cappadocia, Asia, and Bithynia

Peter writes to believers who are to be found in Pontus, Galatia, Cappadocia, Asia, and Bithynia. Two separate countries, Bithynia and Pontus were combined into one senatorial province by Emperor Augustus, an arrangement that goes back to the times of Julius Caesar (d. 44 B.C.), who placed the two countries under one governor. Senatorial provinces were more settled than those designated imperial provinces, which had their governors appointed by the emperor. As their name implies, senatorial provinces had their governors appointed by the Roman Senate. The province of Bithynia et Pontus stretched along the Black Sea, in what is today the northern part of Turkey.

Cappadocia was an imperial Roman province that was south of Bithynia et Pontus, while Galatia was an imperial Roman province to the west of Bithynia and also south of Bithynia et Pontus. Paul's missionary journeys took him to Galatia (Acts 16:6; 18:23), and one of the letters he wrote that was later included in the New Testament is addressed to the Galatians. The Roman provinces of Bithynia et Pontus, Cappadocia, and Galatia all lie within the region known in ancient and modern times as Anatolia or Asia Minor. Today Anatolia is a substantial part of modern Turkey.

How to read 1 and 2 Peter

Almost all of the following sections of this book are based on a passage from 1 or 2 Peter, and you will get the most out of the book if you read that passage from your own Bible before reading what is said about it. As you read, one of the challenges you will find is that some of the sentences are very long in both 1 and 2 Peter. For example, 1 Peter 1:3–12 is one long sentence. Different languages have different ways of expressing ideas. In English, writers are encouraged to break up long sentences to make the ideas easier to follow. But this is not the case with first-century Greek. In fact, good-quality Greek used long sentences, and 1 and 2 Peter are written in excellent Greek. Even in translations that tend to break longer sentences into smaller sentences, many long sentences can be found in 1 and 2 Peter. This does not necessarily mean that it is harder to read. Long sentences in Greek are broken up into lots of smaller components expressing one idea (clauses), and most of the clauses are short. What happens, though, is that these short ideas are linked together to create a larger thought. The result is like a cascade of ideas, all linked together. Reading 1 and 2 Peter, then, is a matter of reading and understanding each of these smaller sections of the sentence, and then combining them into larger units that make up the complete thought of a sentence.

Silvanus

What was the role played by Silvanus?[3] First Peter 5:12 says, "By Silvanus . . . I have written briefly to you" (RSV). In today's world of computers or ballpoint pen and paper, it is common to write your own letters. But in the first century, writing was not so straight forward, and it was usually the case that letters were dictated to a scribe, who would then be responsible for putting together a good copy of the letter. Paul himself used this process. For example, we know that Romans was written down by a scribe called Tertius (Romans 16:22), because Tertius identifies himself and includes his own greeting at the end of the letter. It is possible that Silvanus contributed to the formation of Peter's letter and is responsible for the good quality of the Greek used.[4]

1 Peter 1:2-12: Father, Son, and Holy Spirit

A typical Greek letter starts with the name of the sender and recipient (the *prescript*), and then makes a statement of thanks that includes a petition to God (the *prooemium*).[5] The prescript need not include anything but the name of the writer and recipient(s). Yet Peter adds to his prescript an extended description of those who receive his letter that includes the mention of God the Father, the Spirit, and Jesus Christ (1 Peter 1:2).

Peter follows the *prescript* with the *prooemium*, which extends from verses 3 to 12 in chapter 1 of his letter. One typical English translation breaks 1 Peter 1:3–12 into six sentences; the editors of the United Bible Societies' Greek New Testament, into three. Yet in Greek all the subunits of the sentence (the clauses) are linked together, and 1 Peter 1:3–12 is in fact one long sentence![6] This seemingly mundane observation should alert the reader that there is one continuous flow of thought that runs through these verses.

The content of 1 Peter 1:3–12 revolves around God the Father (verses 3–7a), Jesus (verses 7b–9), and the Holy Spirit (verses 10–12). The *prooemium* begins by praising God the Father for

1. giving a new birth into a living hope (verse 3b);
2. providing an inheritance in heaven (verse 4); and
3. providing protection through the trials that are bringing suffering (verses 5–7a).

Verses 7b through 12 then consider Jesus and the Holy Spirit from the perspective of the readers of the letter, highlighting Their importance in the scheme of salvation and the resultant blessings that Christians have received. Of Jesus it is said that even though they "do not see him now," they

1. love Him (verse 8a);
2. believe in Him (verse 8b);
3. rejoice with indescribable and glorious joy (verse 8c); and
4. receive the outcome of their faith, salvation.

The Holy Spirit is said to have revealed to the prophets the sufferings and subsequent glory of Christ and that the prophets were serving not themselves but those Christians who were reading Peter's letter.

As well as performing its expected task of providing thanks to God and a petition, the long sentence in 1 Peter 1:3–12 also touches on many of the main themes that will recur throughout 1 Peter. It speaks of salvation through the resurrection of Jesus and through the faith of the believer, it looks to the future inheritance of the faithful, and it touches on the persecution experienced by the church members. All these topics will be discussed at length in the letter and in future chapters of this book.

1 Peter 1:13-21: Consequences of salvation

1 Peter 1:13 starts with a word translated as "Therefore" (NIV, NRSV) or "Wherefore" (KJV). The word "Therefore" links what is said in verses 13 through 16 very closely to what has gone before. It has been noted in verses 3 through 12 that Christian believers have been saved through the sacrifice and resurrection of Jesus. They have accepted this salvation by faith. They themselves have not done anything to merit this salvation. God has provided this salvation freely to all through the sacrifice of Jesus.

Yet to accept this salvation has consequences in the lives of the believers. *Because* they have been saved, they will "gird up the loins of [their] mind" (verse 13, KJV). This quaint phrase from the King James Version accurately reflects the underlying idiom in the original Greek of the letter. What it means, though, is perhaps best captured in a modern translation. The New Revised Standard Version, for example, suggests the phrase "gird up the loins of your mind" means "prepare your minds for action."

Peter begins with some examples of what it means to be a Christian. Positively, it means to be sober, to rest fully on grace, and to be obedient children (verses 13, 14). Negatively, it means that Christians should not conform themselves to their inappropriate lusts that dominated their lives before they accepted Christ into their lives. Peter then sums up his thinking by quoting a phrase that occurs often in the book of Leviticus in the Old Testament, "Be holy, for I am holy" (1 Peter 1:16, NRSV; cf. Leviticus 11:44–45; 19:2; 20:7, 26; 21:8). Salvation has been provided to Christians freely, as a gift. Yet *because* they are saved, they will wish to be holy in the sense that God is holy—ethical in all that they do, just in all their judgments, loving to all, even their enemies (cf. Matthew 5:43–48).[7]

First Peter 1:17–20 explores the implications of being a Christian believer in terms of future judgment and redemption through the blood of Christ and faith. There will come a time when God the Father will impartially judge everybody by *what they have done* (verse 17). Thus, what a Christian *does* is important. Not to earn salvation, but because they are saved. What Christians do reveals whether or not they have accepted the free gift of God's salvation. Their relationship with Jesus will inevitably bring changes into their lives; they will reflect the One they worship in who they are *and* what they do.

Peter does not mince his words. An appropriate response to the prospect of future judgment is fear (verse 17). The Greek word used here, *phobō* (from *phobos*), has as its basic meaning "to be afraid." It is a fear of such intensity that it is frequently associated with trembling (e.g., 2 Corinthians 7:15; Ephesians 6:5). In the Old Testament the word also had the idea of "respect" in its usage.[8] One fears and respects the very powerful, and there is none more powerful than God. And it is God that will sit in judgment of our works. The prospect of future judgment is not one to be taken lightly!

Yet while Peter touches on the future judgment in verse 17, he spends much more time on what Jesus has done for the Christian believers: He has "ransomed" them. The New Testament uses a number of words to describe what Jesus has done for us, which all have a meaning in the first-century world beyond the religious sphere. *Justification*, for example, is a term associated with a verdict of "not guilty" in a court of law. *Redemption* means to purchase back. *Salvation* conveys at least two meanings—to rescue somebody from dire danger, or to heal them from illness.[9] *Ransomed*, the term used in 1 Peter 1:18 (NRSV), meant then what it means today—to purchase the freedom of somebody with a payment. Christians were being held captive by sin (and the devil), and Jesus paid the price to free them from captivity. It was a very costly price, that of His own blood. Peter then compares the death of Jesus to a sacrifice. In the Old Testament, sacrifices had to be without defect or blemish (e.g., Leviticus 22:20, 21, 24; 23:12; Numbers 28:11, 19, 31; 29:23; Deuteronomy 15:21; 17:1). They were offered for a variety of reasons, including sacrifices that provided atonement for sin (Numbers 6:11; 15:28; 1 Chronicles 6:49; 29:21). Peter's point is clear: the death of Jesus provided a means of ransoming His people from sin and made atonement for it.

1 Peter 1:22-2:3: Love

Peter had heard the words spoken by Jesus, who plainly told His disciples, "By this all will know that you are My disciples, if you have love for one another" (John 13:35 NKJV), and this is a part of Jesus' teaching that has taken deep root in Peter's thinking. Indeed, love is a theme that Peter returns to often in his first letter (1 Peter 1:8, 22; 2:17; 3:8; 4:8; 5:14; cf. 2 Peter 1:7).

For Peter, the result of "obeying the truth" (1 Peter 1:22, NKJV) is not found in people who are critical of themselves and others. No, "purifying our souls in obeying the truth" results in a "genuine mutual love" (NRSV) or "sincere love of the brethren" (NKJV), which is perhaps a more literal translation of the Greek word used (*philadelphian:* a combination of *philia,* "like/love" and *adelphos,* "brother/sister"). Christians are to "love one another deeply from the heart" (NRSV). The verb here translated as "love" is *agapēsate* (a form of the verb *agapaō*). This is the self-sacrificing kind of love that Jesus says could lead someone to lay down one's life for a friend (John 15:13)[10]—the type of love that Jesus has for lost humanity. This is the ultimate result of truly dedicating oneself to following the truth found in Jesus: a group of believers who are remarkable for their love for one another.

---

1. See "Paul's letters and other ancient Greek letters," in David G. Horrell, *An Introduction to the Study of Paul*, 2nd ed. (London: T&T Clark, 2006), 49, 50. Many ancient letters survive. See, for example, the letters to Diogenes and to Sarapammon in S. R. Lleweylin and J. R. Harrison, eds., *A Review of the Greek and Other Inscriptions and Papyri Published Between 1988 and 1992*, New Documents Illustrating Early Christianity, vol. 10 (Macquarie University, NSW, Australia: Ancient History Documentary Research Centre, 2012), 164, 165, 170–72. As M. Eugene Boring observes, "A letter is a written document . . . [that] spans the distance between people who are separated, and who would communicate directly if possible. . . . A letter is particular and personal . . . a letter adopts or accommodates itself to cultural forms. The author of 1 Peter could have composed a sermon and had it read in the congregations of Asia Minor provinces. The content may have been essentially the same, but this would not have been a letter. . . . 1 Peter qualifies as a real letter on all counts." "Narrative Dynamics in First Peter: The Function of Narrative World," in Robert L. Webb and Betsy Bauman-Martin, eds., *Reading First Peter with New Eyes: Methodological Reassessments of the Letter of First Peter* (London: T&T Clark, 2007), 13.

2. Karl Ludwig Schmidt, διασπορά, in Gerhard Kittle, ed., *Theological Dictionary of the New Testament* (Grand Rapids, MI: Eerdmans, 1964), 2:99.

3. Silvanus is usually identified as the same individual as Silas, a prophet (Acts 15:32) and sometime companion of Paul (Acts 15:40; 17:1–5, 10; 18:5). Paul speaks of Silvanus as a fellow preacher (2 Corinthians 1:19) and as joint author of two of his earliest letters (1 and 2 Thessalonians 1:1). Grant R. Osborn, in Grant R. Osborne and M. Robert Mulholland Jr., *James, 1–2 Peter, Jude, Revelation,* Cornerstone Biblical Commentary, vol. 18 (Carol Stream, IL: Tyndale House, 2011), 265–266.

4. Such in the conclusion of J. N. D. Kelly, *A Commentary on the Epistles of Peter and of Jude* (London: Black, 1969), 214, 215. Kelly considers the possibility that the words used of Silvanus mean that he was the one who was to carry the letter around (cf. Acts 15:23) but rejects it on the grounds that "I have written briefly" means the process of writing, not publishing.

5. See Horrell, "Paul's letters and other ancient Greek letters," 49, 50.

6. Karen H. Jobes, *1 Peter,* Baker Exegetical Commentary on the New Testament (Grand Rapids, MI: Baker Academic, 2005), 109; and Paul J. Achtemeier, *1 Peter,* Hermeneia (Minneapolis: Fortress, 1996), 90, also comment that 1 Peter 1:3–12 is one long sentence. Achtemeier uses the title *Prooemium* for the section of his commentary dealing with 1 Peter 1:3–12.

7. Clifford A. Barbarick summarizes his understanding of being holy as God is holy in the following manner: "The Christian community will he conformed to the holiness of God, understood in terms of the pattern of Christ, through the empowerment of the living and enduring word of God." "You Shall Be Holy, For I Am Holy: Theosis in 1 Peter" *Journal of Theological Interpretation* 92 (2015): 297.

8. See evidence provided in the *Theological Dictionary of the New Testament,* 9:197, 198.

9. These terms, and others, are discussed in Robert K. McIver, "Pauline Images of Salvation." *Ministry* 64, no. 5 (May 1991): 11–13.

10. See discussion on the subtle differences between *phileō,* "I like/love," and *agapaō,* "I love," in endnote 7 in chapter 1.

A Royal Priesthood

1 Peter 2:1-10

In 1 Peter 2:1–10 Peter calls his readers a chosen race, a royal priesthood, a holy nation, and God's own people (verse 9), and much of this chapter will be devoted to discovering why he should feel entitled to use these terms—which applied to the descendants of Abraham in the Old Testament—for Christians. Peter's statement in verse 9 is preceded by a portrayal of Christians as living stones, being built into a structure that has Jesus as its Cornerstone, which he sees as the natural consequence of living as a true Christian.

1 Peter 2:1-3: Living as a Christian

The word translated as "therefore/wherefore" in 1 Peter 2:1, like its use in 1 Peter 1:13, indicates that what Peter is about to say flows out of what has just been said. In 1 Peter 2:1–3, he begins to spell out what it means to be "purified" and to "have genuine mutual love" (1 Peter 1:22, NRSV). Such people, Peter urges, will rid themselves of all malice, guile, insincerity, envy, and slander. Furthermore, with the same passion as a newborn baby, they would long for pure *logikos* milk.

If you compare several translations, you will see that translators have struggled to capture the meaning of the key Greek word *logikos* in English (e.g., "milk *of the word*," NKJV; "*spiritual* milk,"

NIV). The word *logikos* is related to the word *logos* or "word," but it has a slightly wider meaning, including "rational" or "spiritual" (it is translated "spiritual" in Romans 12:1, NRSV). In using this word, Peter is saying that Christians long to be spiritually nourished. He doesn't explicitly identify the nature of the pure spiritual milk, but elsewhere he directs our attention to Scripture, particularly its prophetic insights (1 Peter 1:10–12; 2 Peter 1:16–20). In the following verses he also directs our attention to Jesus Christ, the Living Stone (1 Peter 2:4–8). He is therefore urging that Christians long for a knowledge of Jesus that they may discover by earnestly seeking it in the Scriptures.

1 Peter 2:4-8: Jesus, the Living Stone

In 1 Peter 2:4–8, Peter builds on an image that Jesus used of Himself, that of the stone that the builders rejected, which became the chief cornerstone (Matthew 21:42; Mark 12:10, 11; Luke 20:17, 18; the citation is from Psalm 118:22–24; cf. 1 Peter 2:6, 7).

By coming to Jesus, the Living Stone, Christians themselves are urged, as living stones, to build themselves into a spiritual house (1 Peter 2:5).[1] Peter underlines that he is using a metaphor here. Just as literal stones can be built into a literal house, so Christians (living stones), can be built into a spiritual house (a community of believers, or a church).

Here is something important: Christians do not exist in isolation; rather, they exist in a community of faith. Baptism in the New Testament is a gateway into community, and the spiritual gifts of those baptized are to be used to build up the body of Christ (Ephesians 4:4, 11–15). The body of Christ is another metaphor for the community of believers or church. Individual Christians contribute to building up the community of faith. Christians, then, have the enormous privilege and responsibility to use their gifts to further the cause of Christ and build up His community. In this way, a remarkable structure will be built, a spiritual house made up of living stones.

First Peter 2:4–8 concludes Peter's thoughts concerning Jesus as the Cornerstone by citing three Old Testament passages that highlight the significance of cornerstones: Isaiah 28:16 is quoted in 1 Peter 2:6; Psalms 118:22 in 1 Peter 2:7; and Isaiah 8:14, 15 in 1 Peter 2:8. Peter then goes on to describe the Christian communities in language that had been used of Israel in the Old Testament: "You are a chosen people, a royal priesthood, a holy nation" (1 Peter 2:9, NIV). To understand how Peter could make such an assertion, we must first understand the nature of the covenant relationship between God and His people as it is described in the Old Testament, and understand that Jesus warned the Jewish leaders that they were at risk of losing their special relationship with God.

God's covenant with His people: Old Testament

The special relationship between God and His people in the Old Testament is encompassed by the term *covenant* (or binding agreement), a theme that provides a unifying thought throughout the historical and prophetic writings. In fact, the whole of Deuteronomy is set out in the manner of a Near Eastern vassal treaty (or covenant), a crucial part of which are the blessings if the terms of the covenant are kept and the penalties (or cursings) for a breach of the covenant.[2] In Deuteronomy 27:11–29:1, Moses stipulates that when the tribes have entered the Promised Land, they should arrange themselves, half on the mount of blessings (Mount Gerizim) and half on the mount of cursings (Mount Ebal). A succession of curses and blessings will then be declared, cursings if the covenant is broken, and blessings if it is kept. Joshua 8:30–35 records that in fact, the tribes did read the blessings and cursings between Mount Gerizim and Mount Ebal when they entered the land.

Both 1 and 2 Kings and 1 and 2 Chronicles see the eventual destruction of Israel and Judah as judgments of God. Their sinfulness brought upon them the judgment of God as He enforced the cursings of the covenant (e.g., 2 Chronicles 36:14–21). From the point of view of the writer(s) of 1 and 2 Kings, all of the kings of Israel and most of the kings of Judah did evil, and thereby earned the judgment that God brought upon the two nations.[3]

The message of the prophets prior to the Babylonian invasion was clear-cut. Judah was in danger, because it had forsaken the covenant with God (e.g., Isaiah 24:5; Jeremiah 11:1–13; Hosea 8:1). God's message to His people after they had been removed from the Promised Land and were in exile in Babylonia was that they should renew their covenant with Him to keep His laws and become His people (Isaiah 56:4, 6, 8; Ezekiel 16:61–63).

All this provides the background to the words of Jesus, and later those found in 1 Peter 2:1–10. The Old Testament documents how God's special people have turned their backs on His covenant in the past, and He has punished them. The question Jesus asks in the parable of the wicked tenants is this: If He has punished His people so severely in the past for forsaking His covenant, what will God do if they reject His prophets and murder His only Son?

Matthew 21:43: The kingdom will be given to another

In the parable of the wicked tenants (Matthew 21:33–45; Mark 12:1–12; Luke 20:9–19), Jesus described how a landowner planted a vineyard. But when he sent servants to collect his share of the produce, some were beaten, others killed. Finally, he sent his son, who was also killed. When Jesus asked His audience what would happen to the vineyard, He was told by His listeners that it should be taken from the wicked tenants and given to another.

How should the parable be understood? Most interpreters consider the parable of the wicked tenants in Matthew 21:33–45 to be best understood as an allegory (something not true of many other parables). They point to Isaiah 5:1–7, which portrays the "house of Israel, and the people of Judah" (NRSV) as a vineyard.[4] The owner of the vineyard is understood to be God; the servants to be the prophets; and the son to be Jesus, who was killed.

But what is meant by the taking away of the vineyard from the evil tenants and it being given to another? Jesus says, "The kingdom of God will be taken away from you and given to a people that produces the fruits of the kingdom" (Matthew 21:43, NRSV). As the Gospel writers observe, the chief priests and Pharisees realized that Jesus was speaking about them (verse 45).

Who or what is the "people that produces the fruits of the

kingdom" that Jesus refers to in verse 43? The New Testament is clear that this "new people" is the church.[5] This connection is made elsewhere in Matthew (e.g., Matthew 13:24–30, 36–43, 47–49). In other words, according to the New Testament, the special relationship that God had with the descendants of Abraham now belongs to His new people, those who are followers of Jesus. In the parable of the wicked tenants, Jesus highlights the reasons for the shift in this special relationship. Nor, considering the terms of the original covenant, should such an eventuality be a surprise. It is all the more appropriate, then, for Peter to take up the language of chosen people, priesthood, and people of God to apply them to the Christian church (1 Peter 2:9). By doing so, Peter is claiming that the special relationship that God had with His people in the Old Testament now belongs to the followers of Jesus.[6]

1 Peter 2:5, 9, 10: Chosen race, royal priesthood, God's own people

The terms "chosen race" (Genesis 18:19; Deuteronomy 7:6), "royal priesthood,"[7] and "God's own people" (Isaiah 51:15, 16; Hosea 2:21–23) come from the terms of honor that were used in the Hebrew Bible to describe the special relationship that God had with the descendants of Abraham. These terms of honor now apply to Christians. Becoming a follower of Jesus means being part of His church. It means a special relationship with God that can be described as belonging to a "royal priesthood."

Peter points out that this special relationship is for a special purpose. Christians are to "proclaim the excellencies of him who called you out of darkness into his marvelous light" (1 Peter 2:9, ESV). Christians, then, are called to share their experience of God with others. Jesus has called them from a life in darkness to a life that is in light.

Jesus gave His life to save us from our sins and, in doing so, made provision for the entire world to be saved. As with Israel of old, the terms of honor are also terms of responsibility. Christians have an extraordinary high status—that of the people of God. But this brings the responsibility to invite others to share the high status. As Peter states in verse 10, Christians now form their own people. They once were not a people but now have received mercy to become a people. As a "royal priesthood," Christians have a particularly close relationship with God. But this is not a selfish relationship, which means that they only have the privilege of greater knowledge of and closeness to God. Christians also have the duty to represent God to the people of the world. In the Bible, *holy* usually has the meaning "set aside for the purpose of worship." Therefore, as a "holy" nation, Christians are separated from the world. They live their life according to high moral values. They live a life of loving others. But as they do so, they are like a fire on a cold night that will draw others to its warmth. Christians are tasked with the responsibility of sharing with others the glorious salvation of which they have partaken.

---

1. Charles Bigg notes that the verb *oikodomeisqe* ("be built up") in verse 5 may be in either the indicative mood (a mood used to make statements) or the imperative mood (a mood used to make commands or to exhort strongly). He suggests, rightly I think, that from 1 Peter 1:13 onwards, the sentences have been built around a succession of verbs in the imperative mood (*elpisate,* "set all your hope," verse 13; *genēthēte,* "become, be," verse 15; *anastraphēte,* "behave, conduct yourselves," verse 17; *agapēsate,* "love," in verse 22). The verb *oikodomeisqe* should also be considered to be in the imperative mood and interpreted as an exhortation to build oneself into a living temple. In the indicative mood, *oikodomeisqe* would make a statement of fact and thus be translated as "are being built." *A Critical and Exegetical Commentary on the Epistles of St. Peter and St. Jude* (Edinburgh, Scotland: T&T Clark, 1902), 128.

2. See, for example, Peter C. Craigie, *The Book of Deuteronomy* (Grand Rapids, MI: Eerdmans, 1976), 22–24.

3. All of the kings of Israel and Judah are evaluated in 1 and 2 Kings one of two ways. They either did evil in the sight of the Lord, or they did right in the eyes of the Lord. Interestingly enough, after David (whose heart was "perfect with the Lord"; 1 Kings 15:3, KJV) and Solomon, a positive judgment is only given to kings of Judah, and only eight of the twenty receive it (Asa, Jehoshaphat, Jehoash, Amaziah, Azariah, Jotham, Hezekiah, and Josiah). Evaluations of the kings of Israel: 1 Kings 13:33–34; 14:20; 15:26–30, 34; 16:9, 10, 19, 23–26, 30; 22:51, 52; 2 Kings 1:17; 3:1–3; 9:22–24; 10:28–31, 36; 13:1, 2, 10, 11; 14:23, 24; 15:8–10; 15:13, 14; 15:17, 18, 23–25, 27, 28; 17:1–6. Evaluations of the kings of Judah: 1 Kings 14:21, 22; 15:1–3; 15:11, 14; 22:41–43; 2 Kings 8:16–18; 8:25–27; 9:27, 28; 11:1–13; 12:1–3, 20; 14:1–3; 15:1–5; 15:32–35; 16:1–3, 8; 18:1–3; 21:1–3, 19–23; 22:1, 2; 23:31, 32; 23:36, 37; 24:8, 9; 24:18, 19.

4. See, e.g., W. D. Davies and Dale C. Allison Jr., *A Critical and Exegetical Commentary on the Gospel According to Saint Matthew* (Edinburgh, Scotland: T&T Clark, 1997), 3:177, 178.

5. In "The Sitz im Leben of the Gospel of Matthew," in David R. Bauer and Mark Allen Powell, eds., *Treasures New and Old: Recent Contributions to Matthean Studies* (Atlanta, GA: Scholars, 1996), 30–32, Donald Hagner finds the passages in Matthew "referring to a transference of the Kingdom from Israel to those who believe (the Church)" the "most conspicuous" evidence showing the tension between Israel and the church. Cf. also the remarks of Jack Dean Kingsbury: "Because Israel has repudiated its Messiah, God, claims Matthew, has withdrawn his kingdom from it and given it to the church (21:43) . . . the church is the new 'nation' God has raised up for himself (21:43)"; so Kingsbury, *Matthew,* 2nd ed., Proclamation Commentaries (Philadelphia: Fortress, 1986), 82. Cf. Matthias Konradt, *Israel, Kirche und die Völker im Matthäusevangelium*, WUNT 215 (Tübingen, Germany: Mohr Siebeck, 2007), 199, 347.

6. Betsy Bauman-Martin uses the term *supersession* to describe this claim of 1 Peter. She also notes, "The supersessionism of 1 Peter has largely been ignored, downplayed or denied, but rarely discussed." She goes on to say, "The levels of competition in other texts from the time of 1 Peter indicate more than a respectful sharing or a simple 'sibling rivalry' between fledgling Christianity and recognizable Jewish ideas but a sort of zero-sum game. Some ideas were clearly not sharable. God can have only one chosen people, one plan of salvation, one set of sacred symbols and one canon of sacred texts. What the Petrine author and others ultimately assert is a form of triumphalism based on *critical differences* of belief." "Speaking Jewish: Postcolonial Aliens and Strangers in First Peter," in Webb and Bauman-Martin, *Reading First Peter with New Eyes*, 150, 156.

7. "Royal priesthood" is something that could not exist in the Old Testament, because the priesthood was granted to Aaron and his sons in perpetuity (Exodus 40:12–15), while rulers were to come from the tribe of Judah (Genesis 49:10). Peter's combination of *royal* and *priesthood* represents a startling new status bestowed on Christians—that of royalty, and that of mediator to God. Formerly two separate functions restricted to two special groups of people of high status are now combined into one and something that is true of all Christians.

CHAPTER 4

Social Relationships

1 Peter 2:11-3:7

Christianity is a very practical religion, and in his letter, Peter tackled some of the thorny issues facing the early church. The issues that concerned him have a curiously modern feel about them: how Christians should relate to an oppressive and corrupt society, how to cope with bad employers, and how men and women should live together as husband and wife. Society has changed. In the first century the relationship between employer and employee was usually that of master and slave, and the roles available to women were quite restricted. But much of what Peter says will resonate with many contemporary readers.

1 Peter 2:13-17: The role of government

Peter urges his readers to "conduct [themselves] honorably among the Gentiles" and to "accept the authority of every human institution, whether of the emperor as supreme, or of governors, as sent by him" (1 Peter 2:11, 13, 14; NRSV). In saying this, Peter is not revealing himself to be an unrealistic optimist. After all, at the end of the letter, he sends greeting from "she who is in Babylon" (1 Peter 5:13, NIV). That Peter is indicating "the church in Rome sends their greetings" is universally acknowledged.[1] Peter considers himself to be writing from "Babylon," the terrible persecutor and final destroyer of the nation of Judah (e.g., 2 Kings

25:1–26; 2 Chronicles 36:15–23; Isaiah 21:1–10; 47:1–15; Jeremiah 27:1–22; 50:1–51:58) and a ready-made symbol of all that is evil in the world (cf. Revelation 17:3–5).

There was indeed much that was evil about the Roman Empire. It exercised ruthless power, torturing and killing those that fell afoul of her armies and courts. This power enabled individuals to amass enormous fortunes at the expense and misery of others. For example, through legal and illegal means, a provincial governor was able to amass 1,000,000 sesterces a year. The enormous buying power represented by this wealth is shown by the fact that the normal salary of a day laborer during this period was approximately 1–3 sesterces a day; an unskilled slave could be purchased for 600 sesterces and maintained for between 350 and 500 sesterces a year; and a Roman soldier earned approximately 900 sesterces a year (although this was often supplemented by plunder in times of war).[2] Governors amassed great wealth, and the leading families in Rome were fabulously wealthy. A Roman senator, for example, required a minimum wealth of 1,000,000 sesterces to be able to continue serving in the Senate. They lived in an honor-based society and were in constant competition with each other, often invoking lengthy high-risk legal processes and outright violence against rivals. But aside from these few constraints, there was very little to stop wealthy Romans from all kinds of oppressive behavior. Roman society was riddled with behavior that would be considered corruption and nepotism in the modern world.

A further factor is the persecution of Christians that was currently taking place in the very churches to which Peter was writing (e.g., 1 Peter 3:13–17). This persecution, while sporadic and regional for most of the first century, often took place with the compliance or active participation of the governing authorities.

Why, then, given all that he knew about the Roman Empire, should Peter urge his readers to accept the authority of the emperor and governors (1 Peter 2:13, 14)? Peter does not leave us in doubt. The Roman government, for all its evils, was effective "in punishing evildoers" and maintaining civil order (see verse 14). Roman government was effective in increasing the well-being of the population that lived under it, especially compared to the alternatives. The empire was at war during most of its existence, but these wars rarely took place within its borders. Peace, even an uneasy peace, is better than war. The Romans built roads, mainly for the convenience of their armies. They instituted a cash-based economy, again, mainly for the convenience of supplying armies on their borders from taxes collected elsewhere in the empire. These factors, together with much free trade, allowed a flourishing economy, which fed many more people than would otherwise have been possible. Not everybody was fed, but more survived than at other periods in history. Christians and others living in the first century lived in a very precarious world. Their lives could be forfeit for all kinds of reasons—disease, famine, war. As a consequence, life expectancy was low. It is estimated that life expectancy at birth was from twenty-three to twenty-five years. Less than half of these babies would survive to ten years of age. But those babies hardy enough and lucky enough to be still alive at ten year of age could expect to live a further thirty-six to thirty-eight years.[3] Yet, despite all this, the population within the regions under control of the empire continued to grow throughout most of its existence.

Peter and those he wrote to knew the alternative to strong government—anarchy. We are fortunate to live in a world today where there are very few places without a strong centralized government that provides for police forces and overall security. Thus, for all its faults, the Roman Empire provided stability. It brought freedom from war. It distributed a harsh justice, but nevertheless, a justice based on the rule of law. Commercial and other contracts were enforceable. It built roads and established a money system to support its military needs, but in doing so, created an environment in which the population was able to grow and prosperity was attained by many. Seen in this light, Peter's comments about government make good sense.

1 Peter 2:18-23: Slaves and masters

First Peter 2:18–23 urges household slaves[4] to obey their masters, even when they are harsh—comparing their experience with the suffering of Jesus.

Christianity began from a movement centered on Jesus, whose ministry activity was largely concentrated in the smaller towns in Galilee and the surrounding districts.[5] The one major city that Jesus is said to have entered was Jerusalem, and it was there that He met His death. But while it began as a rural movement, as it spread around the Roman Empire, Christianity often obtained a foothold in the cities before it spread to the countryside. These cities had widely diverse populations, and among the early converts to Christianity were slaves and women that often lived in households that were otherwise non-Christian.

Slaves were important functionaries in the wealthier households across the Roman Empire. They could take on a number of functions that included some with very significant responsibilities. We hear of several of these types of slaves in the New Testament. For example, Galatians 3:24, 25 makes reference to a *paidagōgos* (translated as "schoolmaster" in the KJV; and "disciplinarian" in the NRSV). A *paidagōgos* was an expensive slave or hired freeman who had the responsibility for a young man from age six through midteens or later. They were responsible for disciplining the child and could use a staff or whip to beat them—a slave beating the children of important and wealthy freeborn families! Among their duties, they ensured that their charges attended to their teachers and were well behaved at all times.[6]

Another function that could be taken by a highly educated and trusted slave was that of steward, or manager. We see the work of such a steward in Luke 16:1–9. He has the delegated authority to conduct significant financial transactions on behalf of his master, without consulting his master. Others slaves could be entrusted with managing substantial wealth for their master (e.g., the five, two, and one talents in Matthew 25:14, 15, 19). In Luke 17:7–10, Jesus speaks of a slave who during the day ploughs or tends sheep, while at night serves at the supper table.

In wealthy households, the master and his wife would have separate personal slaves. They would have a steward to conduct their financial affairs and often one able to read and write to handle correspondence. There would be cooks, servers, guards, gardeners, etc. In Pompeii and Helculaneum it is possible to walk through the substantial remains of the houses of the wealthy. It is fascinating to wander through these ruined houses and imagine them as they were in the first century, full of people all working together to ensure the well-being of the family and the success of their financial and domestic affairs. Most of those individuals would have been slaves.

Both slaves and owners were human, and strong relationships often grew between them. But the fundamental reality underlying all of their interaction was that the slave was property owned by the master, and the master had great freedom of action with regard to the slave. Beatings were not uncommon when a slave displeased the master, and under some circumstances, torture, although this would be rare, because the master would be damaging his own property.

The religious tone of the household was set largely by the (male) head of the house (the *paterfamilias*), and to a lesser extent, by the mistress of the house (usually the wife of the *paterfamilias*). One can see this religious leadership in the centurion Cornelius, who became one of the first Gentiles to be baptized as a Christian. "He was a devout man who feared God with all his household" (Acts 10:2, NRSV). After they responded to Peter's teaching with a manifestation of the Spirit, Peter "ordered them to be baptized" (verse 47, NRSV). Presumably, "them" means that the whole household was baptized and thereby became Christian. But in the cities of the Roman Empire, it was more common for slaves and women to become Christian than it was for heads of households. Furthermore, Christians allowed their daughters to marry non-Christians, an important factor in the spread of Christianity in post-New Testament times.

The role of Christian slaves in a pagan household was challenging. Religious observances were conducted in almost all households in the Roman Empire—often as simple as the dedication to the household gods of the animals to be slaughtered for meat for the next meal. A slave would often be asked to participate in something that he or she may find morally or religiously repugnant.

This background provides a context for Peter's exhortation to

Christian slaves to be obedient to their masters (1 Peter 2:18–22). He points out that it is their duty to do so, not just to the considerate master, but also to the harsh master. There is no merit, he says, in enduring a beating for something that deserved punishment—real merit was enduring an undeserved beating (verses 19, 20). In their suffering they can think of the example of Jesus, who did not retaliate when He was insulted, nor make threats when He suffered (verse 23).

Peter then makes a highly significant statement linking the death of Jesus and the life of Christians. Jesus bore our sins on the cross so that we might die to sin. The Christian lives as one who is dead to sin but alive to righteousness (verse 24).

1 Peter 3:1-7: Wives and husbands

Few parts of the modern world have been untouched by the social revolutions that have followed on the heels of industrialization, the movement of the populations to the cities, various movements of liberation (including that of women's liberation), and advances in technology, including the ability to reliably control female fertility. It takes an act of the imagination to envisage the parameters of first-century domestic life in the Roman provinces of Pontus et Bithynia, Cappadocia, and Galatia. At that time, the vast majority of the population was rural. The household was headed by a husband, who spent almost all of his time and energy producing just enough food to feed himself and his family. His wife's duties revolved around managing the house, cooking, and training younger children. For most of her married life she would have been pregnant or breast-feeding while managing younger children. The "traditional roles" adopted by men and women in these circumstances were seldom questioned—everybody was too busy just surviving!

Among the wealthy leaders in the community, women retained the roles of household management and raising children, although they were assisted in these tasks by slaves of various kinds—cooks, personal slaves, servers, a nurse for younger children, a *paidagōgos* for each male child over the age of six, et cetera. Because the Greek-speaking provinces to which Peter writes were strongly influenced by Greek social mores, the women of wealthy families were quite constrained in their social interactions with those outside the household. For example, Roman women would often participate in the meals—an important part of social interaction among the wealthy—but Greek women of high status rarely did if non-family members were present. Paul had to deal with a situation in Corinth, for example, in which Christian women took advantage of the greater freedom they felt and spoke in public more often and more forcefully than others in the community (including Paul) felt to be socially acceptable (1 Corinthians 14:33–35).

Peter's instruction to wives in 1 Peter 3:1–6 should be seen in the light of the social environment in which the Christians that he was addressing lived. Wives should "accept the authority of" (NRSV) or "be submissive to" (NKJV) their husbands. This, after all, was what society expected of dutiful women. Yet Peter addresses this matter in the context of a Christian wife who might be married to a non-Christian partner, and therefore, living in a state of constant ethics-challenging circumstances. Should she, as is the place of the women of the household, participate in the sacrifice to the household gods of the animals destined for meals later in the day? How should she react to her husband's activities in the light of her newly found moral principles that she has discovered as a follower of Jesus?[7] Peter urges "submission." He also points out that she should conduct herself as Christ would. He suggests that rather than find her beauty in outward things such as hair arrangements, wearing gold, and putting on fine apparel, the believing wife might display the "hidden person of the heart, with the incorruptible beauty of the gentle and quiet spirit" (verse 4, NKJV).[8] Peter suggests that it is this style of life that is most likely to recommend Christianity to the unbelieving husband (verse 1b).

Nor does Peter put all the responsibility of a successful marriage on the wife. Husbands should show consideration to their wives and honor them (verse 7).

Christianity and social change

Both Peter and Paul addressed the issues of obedience to Roman authority, slavery, and the role of women in their writings (1 Peter 2:13–3:7; Romans 13:1–10; Ephesians 5:21–6:9; 1 Corinthians 7:12–16; and Galatians 3:27, 28). Both were socially conservative, urging their followers to obey government, their masters (if they were slaves), and their husbands (if they were married). Yet there were times that Peter and Paul did resist legal authority. For example, in Acts 5:27–29, Peter tells the council, "We ought to obey God rather than men" (KJV). Peter was not prepared to accept human limitations on his right to spread the good news of Jesus.

Paul was conscious that being baptized into Christ overturns many of the usual divisions in society. His society was divided into rigid classes, and slavery had a very substantial presence at almost all levels of private and commercial life. Yet Paul insists that when baptized into Christ, there is no distinction between slave and free. Nor is there a distinction based on race (Galatians 3:28; Colossians 3:11). In an earlier era, there was a special relationship between God and the descendants of Abraham. In Christ there is no distinction between Jew and Gentile. And Paul insists that in Christ there is no distinction between male and female (Galatians 3:28).

Throughout history, Christians have been law-abiding and supportive of their government. In addition, Christians have been at the center of important positive social change. Take, for example, the issue of slavery addressed in 1 Peter 2:18–21. It took a long time, but Christians eventually worked out that owning slaves and allowing others to own slaves was a moral evil. They worked through governments to abolish the slave trade.

At other times, Christians have brought about social change by protesting their treatment by government. Both Gandhi and Martin Luther King Jr. were able to change deeply entrenched social inequalities by applying the council of Jesus, who urged His followers not to return violence with violence (Matthew 5:38–42). In other words, that Christians are supportive and obedient to governments does not mean that they should not work to improve the standards of society.

The challenge for Christians then and now is to work out when it is appropriate to stay within the conventional social framework in which they find themselves or whether it is now time to challenge wider society with the extra ethical insight that comes with being a Christian. The "Serenity Prayer" used by Reinhold Niebuhr in a 1943 sermon is one that many Christians find resonates with their position in society, as well as in their personal lives:

> God, give me grace to accept with serenity
> the things that cannot be changed,
> Courage to change the things
> which should be changed,
> and the Wisdom to distinguish
> the one from the other.
>
> Living one day at a time,
> Enjoying one moment at a time,
> Accepting hardship as a pathway to peace,
> Taking, as Jesus did,
> This sinful world as it is,
> Not as I would have it,
> Trusting that You will make all things right,
> If I surrender to Your will,
> So that I may be reasonably happy in this life,
> And supremely happy with You forever in the next.
>
> Amen.

---

1. E.g., Douglas Harink, *1 & 2 Peter* (Grand Rapids, MI: Bazos, 2009), 130; Francis D. Nichol, ed., *The Seventh-day Adventist Bible Commentary* (Washington, DC: Review and Herald®, 1957), 7:589.

2. John Dominic Crossan has provided a useful summary of social and economic aspects of the Roman Empire in his book *The Birth of Christianity* (San Francisco: HarperSanFrancisco, 1998), 178–182, 215–235.

3. See the life tables in Robert K. McIver, *Memory, Jesus, and the Synoptic Gospels* (Atlanta, GA: Society of Biblical Literature, 2011), 189–202. See also

Jonathan L. Reed, "Instability in Jesus' Galilee: A Demographic Perspective," *Journal of Biblical Literature* 129 (2010); 343–365.

4. The word translated as "servant" or "slave" in 1 Peter 2:18, *oiketai* (a form of the noun *oiketēs*), is used specifically for domestic slaves. It is found only four times in the New Testament, at 1 Peter 2:18; Luke 16:13; Acts 10:7; Romans 14:4; but cf. *oiketeias* in Matthew 24:45 (*Logos* Bible Software, Biblical Languages Package). The more usual word for slave, *doulos* (used 126 times in the New Testament according to *Logos*), is used in Ephesians 6:5, part of a passage that gives similar advice to slaves to that found in 1 Peter 2:18–23.

5. The capitol of Galilee for most of His youth was Sepphoris, a city a mere six kilometers from Nazareth. As Joseph and Jesus were carpenters, and given that Nazareth was a very small town indeed, Joseph and Jesus almost certainly worked there on the major reconstruction and construction projects that took place at Sepphoris at this time. See Robert K. McIver, "Sepphoris and Jesus: Missing Link or Negative Evidence?" in David Merling, ed., *To Understand the Scriptures: Essays in Honor of William H. Shea* (Berrien Springs, MI: Institute of Archaeology, Andrews University, 1997), 221–232. The other major population center and city in Galilee, Tiberius, is mentioned in the New Testament, but Jesus is never said to have entered it.

6. See the fascinating description of the work of a *paidagōgos* in Norman H. Young, "*Paidagogos*: The Social Setting of a Pauline Metaphor," *Novum Testamentum* 29 (1987): 150–176; and Norman H. Young, "The Figure of the *Paidagōgos* in Art and Literature," *Biblical Archaeologist* 53 (June 1990): 80–86. The 1990 article includes photographs of figurines and Greek pottery that portray a *paidagōgos*.

7. "We can conclude from the author's remark 'even if some of them do not obey the word' that many of the women being addressed are married to non-Christians. Thus, the exhortation to the wives to submit is similar to the exhortation to the slaves; it encourages them to accept their husbands' authority during the persecution that they face as a result of their disobedience. Their independent conversions, attendance at Christian meetings, and neglect of their cultic duties all constituted a crossing of boundaries that subverted the authority of the paterfamilias and forced them to negotiate between two communities in conflict. It is that subversion that the author encourages when he tells the wives to 'do what is good' (ἀγαθοποιοῦσαι) even if the consequences are frightening (3:11)." So writes Betsy J. Bauman-Martin, "Women on the Edge: New Perspectives on Women in the Petrine *Haustafel*," *Journal of Biblical Literature* 123 (2004): 273.

8. In her fascinating article, "Neither Gold nor Braided Hair (1 Timothy 2.9; 1 Peter 3.3): Adornment, Gender and Honour in Antiquity," *New Testament Studies* 55 (2009), 484–501, Alicia J. Batten notes that "the exhortations not to braid hair, wear gold pearls or expensive clothes are consistent with the general Graeco-Roman male emphasis upon female modesty and criticism of

female adornment . . . they are standard tropes" (p. 497). She documents many comments from antiquity that are consistent with what is said in 1 Peter 3:3 and 1 Timothy 2:9, both in religious texts such as the first-century BCE Rule of the Andanian Mysteries and in satirical plays and other texts. She also points out that from the perspective of a woman, the appearance of her dress and adornment were important indicators of social status in a society that was driven by matters of honor and social standing.

CHAPTER 5

Living for God in Mutual Love

1 Peter 3:8-12, 18, 21; 4:1-11

For Peter, *love* lies at the core of the Christian experience (1 Peter 1:8), *love* is the goal of faith (2 Peter 1:5, 6), and *love* is characteristic of interactions between Christians (1 Peter 1:22; 2:17; 3:8). This chapter explores some of the practical implications of the genuine mutual love that believers should have for one another.

Loving someone means caring enough about them to wish their good and acting in a manner that enhances the likelihood of increasing that good. Blind acceptance of anything somebody else does is not love, it is indifference. Unconditional love is not like that. Take, for example, the love of a mother for her child. A mother loves her child unconditionally, while at the same time clearly seeing her child's weaknesses and strengths. She will always wish the best for her child and work unceasingly to bring it about. It is the same with our Christian brothers and sisters. We accept each other as Christ has accepted us—unconditionally. But that does not mean that we cease to care what each other does. We care so much that we not only would wish to rejoice on what is working well in their lives but also would wish to warn them of potential dangers.

In this chapter we'll look at passages where Peter talks about how Christians should relate to each other, particularly in areas where there are social problems. It explores what he says about two potential dangers in the ancient world that are still problematic for today: the abuse of alcohol and sexual license. What he says about those topics needs to be framed in his wider perspective on how Christians should care for each other, found in 1 Peter 3:8–11.

1 Peter 3:8-11: Unity of spirit

In 1 Peter 2:18–3:7, Peter has been giving advice to two specific groups: slaves and spouses. He now finishes his sequence by giving advice that everybody should heed: "Finally, all of you, have unity of spirit" (1 Peter 3:8 NSRV).

What is meant by "unity of spirit"? Paul provides valuable insight into how the church functions in unity. In 1 Corinthians 12:1–13:13, he points out that just as the body is made up of things as different as a hand and an eye but still has an intrinsic unity, so, too, the church is made up of individuals with quite different spiritual gifts. Thus unity is not necessarily uniformity. But the ideal of both Paul and Peter is that the varied individuals that make up the church should have unity of spirit. This unity enables the church to function as a whole in fulfilling its mission of representing Jesus to a world that desperately needs to hear of the salvation that Jesus brings.

In some places it must be admitted that the church falls far short of the ideal of unity. Perhaps that should not be surprising, given that churches are made up of fallible human beings. Even so, Peter gives some robust advice that would change that. For example, he says Christians should act with sympathy (1 Peter 3:8). Sympathy means that when one Christian suffers, then others will suffer with them; when another Christian rejoices, other Christians will rejoice with them (compare with 1 Corinthians 12:26). Sympathy enables us to see from another's perspective. This is an important step along the way to unity of spirit. But Peter then says we should have "love for one another" (1 Peter 3:8). Jesus Himself had said that the way you can tell His true disciples is that they have love one for another (John 13:35). Furthermore, Christians, Peter says, will have a tender heart. They will have compassion for each other's difficulties and failings. Finally, Christians will have a humble mind (1 Peter 3;8).

Given these qualities, Christians naturally will not repay evil with evil (verse 9). As is stated in the words of Psalm 34:12–16 (which are quoted by Peter in 1 Peter 3:10–12), they will keep their "lips from speaking deceit," and will "seek peace, and pursue it" (NRSV). Would such a group of Christians have unity of spirit? Surely!

1 Peter 4:1, 2: Ceased from sin

First Peter 3:18, 21 and 4:1, 2 contain within them a succinct statement about the saving work of Jesus and how believers participate in that salvation. Each word of 1 Peter 3:18 is charged with meaning. For example, there is a small word in Greek used in 1 Peter 3:18 that emphasizes the comprehensive nature of Jesus' sacrifice. It is the word *hapax,* which means "once for all." The word is related to the word *ephapax,* "once and for all," found in Romans 6:10; Hebrews 7:27; and 9:12. Peter uses the word *hapax* to emphasize the comprehensive nature of the suffering of Jesus. He says, "Christ also suffered for sins once for all [hapax], the righteous for the unrighteous, in order to bring you to God" (1 Peter 3:18, NRSV).

The phrase "Forasmuch then . . ." (KJV; "Since therefore," NRSV) in 1 Peter 4:1 links what is said in 1 Peter 4:1, 2 with what has just been said in 1 Peter 3:18–22. In these earlier verses, Peter points out that Christ suffered for sins that He might bring us to God (verse 18), and that "baptism doth . . . now save us" (verse 20, KJV). In other words, Peter links the suffering of Jesus and salvation through baptism.

Baptism, then, is perhaps the best context against which to understand Peter's words, "for he that hath suffered in the flesh has ceased from sin" (1 Peter 4:1, KJV; "has finished with sin," NRSV). So as Christians participate in the suffering and death of Jesus by baptism, they then should "live for the rest of [their] earthly [lives] no longer by human desires, but by the will of God" (verse 2, NRSV; cf. Romans 6:1–11).

Paul's words, "reckon ye also yourselves to be dead indeed

unto sin, but alive unto God through Jesus Christ our Lord" (Romans 6:11, KJV), give the secret of the Christian's life. In Christ, a Christian is dead to sin. A Christian should then live out that reality. Or as Peter puts it, "Live for the rest of your earthly life no longer by human desires but by the will of God" (1 Peter 4:2, NRSV).

1 Peter 4:3-6: Problems of the past life A: Alcohol abuse

First Peter 4:3–6 provides a list of things that Peter says characterizes what "Gentiles like to do." For Peter, these types of behaviors are not suitable for Christians, especially in the light God's final judgment (verse 5). It is interesting that several of them involve the misuse of alcohol or sexual impropriety.

The three terms used in 1 Peter 4:3 that relate to alcohol abuse are "revels," "carousings" (NRSV), and "excess of wine" (KJV)/"drunkenness" (NRSV).

Revel (Greek *kōmos*) is a term used to describe a drinking party with music and dancing, and often ended with the party parading through the streets with torches singing and dancing. The word *kōmos* could also be used of festal processions in honor of gods such as Bacchus (the god of alcohol) or in honor of the victor at the games.[1] Alcohol was a very prominent feature of a revel. So much so that it is appropriate to describe a revel as a drunken procession. They are frequently mentioned in ancient written sources and portrayed on pottery vessels and in mosaics.

Carousings (Greek *potos,* plural *potoi*)[2] are drinking parties where much wine was consumed. Information from ancient sources indicates that in the Middle East, wine was often boiled into a concentrate before storage, and then was generally mixed with water. Homer, for example, mentions that wine was mixed in a ratio of twenty parts of water to one part of wine.[3] Later writers give different ratios; ratios of three to five parts of water to one part of wine appear to be the norm. Any ratio that was less than one part of water to one part of wine was considered to be strong wine.[4] Even though the alcohol content of first-century wine was low by modern standards, drinking enough of it will bring about intoxication, and the result of carousing was usually drunkenness.

Drunkenness results from an excessive consumption of alcohol. As a person drinks alcohol, they first lose many of their social inhibitions. This can facilitate social occasions—until the person affected by drink becomes insulting to others. On consuming more alcohol, the drinker then progresses to a state of making very poor judgments, and finally reaches a stage where they lose motor control of their body so much so that they find difficulty in walking a straight line.[5] It is a sad fact that while the majority of people are able to manage their alcohol consumption, about one in ten people who drink regularly will become alcoholics.[6] An alcoholic puts drinking in front of every other social relationship. It is more important to them than friends, their children, and their spouse. Their alcoholism affects not only themselves but also those around them. In many countries, the abuse of alcohol is *the* most important social problem, far eclipsing the evils associated with illegal drugs.

What is the loving response appropriate for Christians to take regarding the problems of alcohol abuse and alcoholism? Wider society struggles to cope with how best to approach these issues, and solutions have yet to be found though many committed and highly intelligent people are working toward finding them. Even so, because love for others lies at the core of their motivation, Christians will not cease working toward educating on the dangers of inappropriate alcohol use. Members of some Christian denominations, and I am proud to belong to one of them, have agreed that they will not drink alcohol at all, out of love to those in their midst who would otherwise become alcoholics.

1 Peter 4:3-6: Problems of the past life B: Inappropriate expressions of sexuality

It is all too easy for Christians to give the wrong impression when discussing sexuality. The Bible is not against sex. In fact, Charles Wittschiebe has succinctly captured the essential message of what the Bible has to say about sex in the title of his book: *God Invented Sex.*[7] In other words, sex is a gift from God. It is one of the key ingredients that binds two married people together in a lifelong commitment and forms the very best foundation for raising children. In its proper place, sexuality is a profound blessing. Yet because sexuality is such a strong part of the human condition, there are many ways in which it can go wrong. From the Gentile world in which his readers lived, Peter highlights several of the pitfalls that can take place regarding sex.

In the list of words of improper things "Gentiles like to do" (verse 3, NSRV), sexual impropriety is explicit in the word translated "lasciviousness" (KJV)/"licentiousness" (NRSV) and implied in the words "lusts" (KJV)/"passions" (NSRV), revels, and banquets. Revels and banquets were notoriously associated with both drunkenness and orgies in the Roman and Greek worlds. Excessive alcohol lowers inhibitions and affects judgment, increasing the likelihood of inappropriate sexual behavior. The word translated "lasciviousness" (*aselgeiais*) is used to describe behavior that is completely lacking in moral constraint, usually with the implication of sexual licentiousness and even acts of violence.[8]

Peter's summary of what is wrong with how sexuality can be expressed also illustrates some of the ingredients of appropriate sexuality and is consistent with moral standards. In particular, it is consistent with the commitment made by a couple as they marry each other and swear before God that they will keep themselves only for each other. Just as casual sex with a stranger or a near stranger that takes place at a revel or banquet is wrong, then appropriate sexuality is associated with a long-term commitment to an exclusive relationship with one spouse. Any children that result from sexual activity will be best nurtured in a long-term relationship of two parents who are committed to Jesus. The vicissitudes of life can lead to the death of a spouse or the breakdown of a marriage. But even in such circumstances, the principles visible in Peter's instruction are clear: sexual expression needs to be guided by the clear instructions found within Scripture and belongs properly to a long-term, exclusive relationship. In this most important and intimate area of love, this is how Christians should act together in mutual love.

1 Peter 4:7-11: Love covers all

First Peter 4:7 states that "the end of all things is near" (NRSV).

Throughout their history, Christians have been comforted and challenged by the expectation of the return of Jesus to this world. Peter points out that this realization will have a significant impact on what Christians do.

First, Christians are to be "sober" (KJV)/"serious" (NRSV; verse 7b). They are not to become alarmists or extreme. Neither are they to use the shortness of time as an excuse for irresponsible behavior. Second, Christians are to discipline themselves to prayer (verse 7c). Prayer will become a natural part of the daily experience of a Christian. Third, Peter urges Christians to be hospitable (verse 9). The Second Coming may be near, but Christians should not withdraw from social relationships because of it. Fourth, when Christians speak, they must do so as one who is speaking the words of God (verse 11). In other words, the seriousness of the time calls for serious communication about spiritual truths.

Finally, and "above all," Christians are to "maintain constant love for one another" (verse 8, NRSV).[9] Peter observes simply that "love covers a multitude of sins" (verse 8b, NRSV). He no doubt agrees with Jesus and Paul, who say that the whole law is summed up in the obligation to love God with our whole heart and love our neighbors as ourselves (Matthew 22:34–39; Mark 12:28–37; Luke 10:25–28; cf. Romans 13:8–10).

---

1. *A Lexicon Abridged From Liddell and Scott's Greek-English Lexicon* (Oxford: Clarendon, 1926), s.v. κῶμος. A revel of torchlight procession could be held after a banquet. For example, it was said of Emperor Domitian that "he gave frequent and sumptuous banquets, but they were short, for he never prolonged them after sunset, and held no revel afterwards." Suetonius, *Lives of the Twelve Caesars,* translated by H. M. Bird (London: Wordsworth Classics, 1997), p. 363, Domitian 21.

2. The King James Version translates *potoi,* "carousings," as "banquetings." Banquets were an important part of social life in the Roman Empire, especially among the elite. They consisted of a lavish amount of food and wine that were provided to important guests (Greek custom was that the wine followed the meal. Katharine Raff, "The Roman Banquet," The Met, October 2011, http://www.metmuseum.org/toah/hd/banq/hd_banq.htm). While banqueting may bring about drunkenness, the word *potoi* in 1 Peter 4:3 has the more specific meaning identified in the main text, and banqueting is not the translation

used by modern translations. The New King James Version translates the word as "drinking parties."

3. Homer, *The Odyssey,* 9.208, 209.

4. These figures are derived from Robert H. Stein's article "Wine-Drinking in New Testament Times," *Christianity Today* 19 (June 20, 1975): 923. The rabbinic literature clearly states that the strong drink mentioned in the Hebrew Bible is undiluted wine (*Jewish Encyclopaedia,* 12:533), although other fermented drinks made from a variety of grains and fruits were known in ancient times. Wine was the preferred alcoholic drink in the Roman Empire.

5. The physical effects of various levels of alcohol consumption are described in John F. Ashton and Ronald S. Laura, *Uncorked! The Hidden Hazards of Alcohol,* 2nd ed. (Warburton, Victoria, Australia: Signs, 2009), 2–8.

6. Peter N. Landless, "Adventists and Alcohol," *Adventist Review,* December 22, 2011, notes that research indicates that "the chance of alcoholism developing over a lifetime is 13 percent (13 people of every 100 who drink alcohol)."

7. Charles E. Wittschiebe, *God Invented Sex* (Nashville, TN: Southern, 1974).

8. Jobes, *1 Peter,* 266, 267.

9. In this verse, as in 1 Corinthians chapter 13, the King James Version translates the Greek word *agapē* as "charity." They probably did so to distinguish their translation of *agapē,* the "highest" type of love, from *philos,* which means the love of a friend. The Greek language had two other words that could be translated with the English word "love": *eros,* sexual love; and *storgē,* the love of a parent for a child. However appropriate the desire of the translators of the King James Version to translate *agapē* by the word "charity" to distinguish it from other types of love expressed by different Greek words, today the meaning of the word *charity* has changed so much that it now does not represent the Greek word *agapē* at all well. Thus most modern translations will use the word "love" in this verse and in 1 Corinthians chapter 13.

CHAPTER 6

Suffering

1 Peter 3:13-22; 4:12-19

Persecution is clearly a present reality in the life of the Christians to whom Peter is writing. In the first chapter, Peter comments that "now for a little while you may have had to suffer various trials . . ." (1 Peter 1:6, NIV), and almost the last comment in the letter also deals with suffering: "And after you have suffered a little while . . ." (1 Peter 5:10, NRSV). Within the short epistle, there are no less than three extended passages that deal with his readers' suffering for Christ (1 Peter 2:19–25; 3:13–21; 4:12–19). By any reckoning, then, the suffering experienced by believers because of their attachment to Christianity is a major theme of 1 Peter. It is to that theme that our attention will be drawn in this chapter.

Persecution of early Christians

In the first-century Roman Empire, various minority groups often found themselves experiencing persecution. For example, Acts 18:2 mentions that Aquila and Priscilla had to leave Rome because Emperor Claudius had ordered all the Jews to leave Rome.[1] In addition, we know of several times when sporadic persecution broke about against Christians in the early years of their existence. For example, Nero (emperor A.D. 54–68) used Christians as convenient scapegoats to punish for a fire that had destroyed a large part of the city of Rome. The Roman historian Tacitus describes this event in his *Annals* 15.38–44. The rumor had circulated that the fire was started by Nero himself:

> Consequently, to get rid of the report, Nero fastened the guilt and inflicted the most exquisite tortures on a class hated for their abominations, called Christians by the populace. Christus, from whom the name had its origin, suffered the extreme penalty during the reign of Tiberius at the hands of one of our procurators, Pontius Pilatus, and a most mischievous superstition, thus checked for the moment, again broke out not only in Judaea, the first source of the evil, but even in Rome, where all things hideous and shameful from every part of the world find their centre and become popular. Accordingly, an arrest was first made of all who pleaded guilty; then, upon their information, an immense multitude was convicted, not so much of the crime of firing the city, as of hatred against mankind. Mockery of every sort was added to their deaths. Covered with the skins of beasts, they were torn by dogs and perished, or were nailed to crosses, or were doomed to the flames and burnt, to serve as a nightly illumination, when daylight had expired.[2]

It was during Nero's reign that both Peter and Paul died as martyrs in Rome.

The cult of emperor worship could be a problem at times for both Jew and Christian alike. Even though they were constantly surrounded by flatterers and sycophants, most of the emperors usually eschewed being elevated to the status of divine being or god, although Caligula (emperor A.D. 37–41) and Domitian (emperor A.D. 81–96) were notable exceptions.[3] Things were different in the Greek-speaking eastern part of the Roman Empire, which had a long history of considering their kings to have divine status. Many requests were sent to different emperors to erect temples in their honor, requests that were often granted. At various times, people were asked to show their loyalty to the empire by sacrificing to the emperor as a god. Polytheists could do this with a clear conscience, though often found it distasteful. Jews were renowned for resisting such requests, even to the point of death. Christians were less well known and sometimes found themselves with very difficult choices when confronted with tests of loyalty that involved such matters as offering incense to the emperor as god or participating in public events in which the emperor was worshiped.

The evidence, sparse though it is, supports the conclusion that Christians living in the Roman Empire could find themselves under significant threat at any time. At times, they, like other minorities, could be dispossessed or killed for just being a Christian. At other times they could be forced to make a decision between personal safety and their faith. When Peter speaks of the trials of Christians to which he writes, he is talking about real danger.

1 Peter 3:13-22: Suffering and the example of Christ

Peter begins with a rhetorical question, "Who will harm you if you are eager to do what is good?" (1 Peter 3:13, NRSV). He then raises the possibility that his readers may suffer for doing what is right. The construction he uses in Greek indicates that the potential for suffering, while real, is likely to be sporadic.[4] He makes several responses to that possibility:

- First, they are blessed because of their suffering (verse 14).
- They should not fear, but they should make the Lord (that is Christ) holy in their hearts (verse 15).
- They should be ready to provide a defense of their hope when required, whether in the law courts or in private one-on-one conversations (verse 15).
- They should keep their conscience clear, so that when they are accused, they will have the confidence that they have done no wrong (verse 16).

Peter concludes that it is better to suffer for doing good,

because Christ Himself suffered for His righteousness (verses 17, 18). But His suffering brought about a way to forgive sins. He died in the place of sinners ("the righteous for the unrighteous," verse 18, NRSV), so that those who believe in Him might be brought to God. "He was put to death in the flesh, but made alive in the spirit, in which also he went and made a proclamation to the spirits in prison" (verses 18b, 19, NRSV).

When exactly did Jesus make a proclamation to the spirits in prison (verse 19), and who were they? Peter elsewhere talks of the resurrection of Jesus, and throughout the rest of his letter appears to share the attitude to death and resurrection that is found elsewhere in the New Testament (see "2 Peter 1:12–15: Putting off the body?" in chapter 9). So it is highly unlikely that he would wish to imply that Jesus made His visit to the spirits in prison as a disembodied ghost. Nor is the rest of Scripture that helpful in determining what Peter was meaning, as there is no discussion of such spirits elsewhere in the books that make up the Bible.[5] My conclusion will be unsatisfactory to some, but I think this is one of the passages in the Bible where we lack key information that would enable us to understand what is meant here.[6]

Peter also cites the example of salvation through water. Just as the ark saved Noah and a few others from destruction by water, so also the water of baptism plays a part in enabling the Christian to appeal to God with a clear conscience (1 Peter 3:21).[7] Jesus, after all, now sits at the right hand of God in heaven in a position of great power (verse 22).

1 Peter 4:12-16: Reactions to persecution

In 1 Peter 4:12, Peter describes the persecution that his readers are experiencing as like a "fiery ordeal," that will "test" them (NIV, NRSV). Fire is a good metaphor for Peter to use. Fire can be destructive, but it can also clean away impurities. It depends on what is experiencing fire—houses are destroyed by fire; silver and gold are purified by fire. Suffering and persecution can have the same effect on the church by revealing those who are truly committed to their Lord.

Yet persecution is not something that should be courted. Peter is adamant about this, both in this passage and in 1 Peter 3:13–22. Peter says that while there is no shame for suffering as a Christian, a Christian should not suffer because they are a murderer, thief, wrongdoer, or mischief maker (1 Peter 4:13).

Christian history shows that as well as refining the church, persecution can also have some highly undesirable outcomes. One example of an undesirable outcome of persecution is the formation of the Donatist movement in northern Africa as a response to the persecution of Christians ordered by Diocletian (a Roman emperor who ruled from A.D. 284 to 305). From the year 303 Diocletian made a systematic attempt to stamp out Christianity, ordering Christian churches and writings destroyed and forcing pagan worship on those who may be Christian. The governor of Africa had been lenient in enforcing these edicts, and those Christians who surrendered the Christian scriptures were considered to have met the requirements of Diocletian. The African Christians were therefore divided into two groups: those who felt that they could surrender Christian writings and those who would not. When the pressure of persecution eased, the church in Africa split into two. One group, called the Donatists, refused to acknowledge baptism and ordination of those who had complied with the government order.[8]

Similar splits within the church as a result of persecution have happened throughout history, and even in modern times. Such divisions are very painful in the church.

1 Peter 4:17-19: Judgment of the people of God

The prophets in the Old Testament were clear that judgment would not come just upon the heathen nations but would come to Israel itself. There are some passages—for example, Isaiah 10:11, 12; Ezekiel 9:1–6; and Malachi 3:1–6—where the process of judgment is portrayed as actually starting with the people of God. It may be this concept that Peter draws upon in 1 Peter 4:17. In this verse, Peter makes a link between the sufferings of his readers and the judgement of God. For him, the sufferings that his Christian readers are experiencing are nothing less than the judgment of God, which begins with the household of God. As both Malachi 3:1–6 and 1 Peter 4:18 warn, God's judgment is not something to be taken lightly. Christians, too, must measure up to the standards of a holy God (1 Peter 1:16). A Christian's life must reflect the call to righteousness from a holy God.

---

1. Acts 18:2 is one of the few places in the book of Acts where cross-references can be made to historical events, which helps those interested in Paul to work out a chronology of his journeys and assists in dating his letters. Or it would be, if Claudius had done this only once, but we know of at least three separate occasions where he expelled all the Jews from Rome.

2. Tacitus, *Annals* 15.44, http://www.earlychristianwritings.com/text /annals.html.

3. Suetonius notes both good and bad about the emperors he describes, and among the long account of Caligula's shortcomings is the complaint that "he ordered all the images of the gods, which were famous either for their beauty or the veneration paid them, among which was that of Jupiter Olympius, to be brought from Greece, that he might take the heads off and put on his own. . . . He also instituted a temple and priests, with choicest victims, devoted to his peculiar worship." Of Domitian, Suetonius recounts, "With equal arrogance, when he dictated the form of a letter to be used by his procurators, he began it thus: 'Our lord and god commands so and so'; when it became a rule that no one should style him otherwise either in writing or speaking." *Lives of the Twelve Caesars,* trans. H. M. Bird (London: Wordsworth Classics, 1997), p. 184, Caligula 22; p. 358, Domitian 13.

4. First Peter 3:14 begins with *all' ei kai* (literally: "but if also") plus a verb in the optative mood (*paschoite*). Wayne Grudem, presumably on the basis of this optative, suggests that "harm is not the normal expectation." *1 Peter*, Tyndale New Testament Commentaries (Grand Rapids, MI: Eerdmans, 1988), 151. I think Paul Achtemeier has better captured the sense of the optative when he suggests that "while the author knows suffering is always a threat, he does not know whether the communities addressed in the letter will be undergoing persecution at the time he is writing, or the time they will read, the letter. To express such a sporadic reality, the author has employed the optative." Achtemeier, *1 Peter*, 231.

5. Possible exceptions are 2 Peter 2:4, Jude 6, and the book of Revelation (e.g., Revelation 6:9, 10). The references in the book of Revelation are in highly symbolic passages that need considerable interpretation. For more on 2 Peter 2:4 and Jude 6, see comments on 2 Peter 2:4–6 in chapter 11.

6. A widely circulated explanation sees the background of the "souls in prison" in some references in 1 Enoch. For example, writing in the very conservative journal, *Journal of the Evangelical Theological Society,* Peter Davids says, "First Peter does mention Noah briefly in 3:20. The reference is so brief that it is difficult to determine which version(s) of the narrative 1 Peter knew.

However, it is clear that the reference to the disobedient spirits that precedes the reference to Noah is drawn from parts of 1 Enoch, while the language applied to Noah fits most closely with Josephus (Ant. 1:72–75). So the 1 Peter version has language and story elements that come from Second Temple literature rather than the Hebrew Scriptures." Peter H. Davids, "What Glasses Are You Wearing? Reading Hebrew Narratives Through Second Temple Lenses," *Journal of the Evangelical Theological Society* 55 (2012): 767. I am not averse to the possibility of finding the influence of 1 Enoch in the New Testament. After all, most everybody who has translated extensive fragments of the Greek version of 1 Enoch as I have (M. Black, ed. *Apocalypsis Henochi Graece* [Leiden: Brill 1970]) reach the near inescapable conclusion that Jude 14, 15 is a loose citation of 1 Enoch 1:9. But even though 1 Enoch deals extensively with the "souls" that resulted from the union of the sons of God with the daughters of men in Genesis 6:1, 2 (e.g., 1 Enoch 6:1–11:2; 15:1–16:3), and he is shown in vision the places where the fallen angels are kept (e.g., 1 Enoch 21:1–23:4; 27:1–4), I cannot persuade myself after reading these passages that this is what is in view in 1 Peter 3:10, although I will argue later that they do form the background of 2 Peter 2:4 (see chapter 11). Hence the rather unsatisfactory conclusion that I think we do not have sufficient background information against which to understand Peter's comment in 1 Peter 3:19 regarding Jesus preaching to the spirits in prison.

7. "The Flood represents God's watery judgment on sinful creation. The Ark safely bore Noah's family . . . through this tide of judgment and wrath. Passing through the waters of baptism is seen as functioning similarly, bearing the faithful through the flood of judgment, and safely through to the other side. All this is rooted in the death and resurrection of Jesus (3:21–22), who spoke of his own crucifixion as baptism (Mark 9:35–40)." So comments Eugene R. Schlesinger, "Fire in the Water: Baptismal Aptness and Ecology in the Petrine Epistles," *Journal of Theological Interpretation* 7 (2013): 281.

8. The Donatists are of sufficient importance to appear in most histories of early Christianity and in many survey histories that try to capture the broad sweep Christian history. See, for example, Everett Ferguson, *Church History Volume One: From Christ to the Pre-Reformation* (Grand Rapids, MI: Zondervan, 2013), 187–190, 274–276; Hans J. Hillerbrand, *A New History of Christianity* (Nashville, TN: Abingdon, 2012), 76–79. Some of the leading ideas of Donatists, and the orthodox church's response to them, may be found in J. N. D. Kelly, *Early Christian Doctrines,* 5th ed. (New York: Harper & Row, 1978), 409–427, 424, 247, 447.

Servant Leadership

1 Peter 5:1-12

Peter addresses the matter of Christian leadership in 1 Peter 5:1–10. Church elders, he says, should be willing to lead, and to do so without considerations of gain. They should not lord it over their charges, but act humbly. They should trust God but remain vigilant against the attacks of the devil.

1 Peter 5:1, 2: The role of elders in the early church

The office of elder has a rich background in Jewish history.[1] Numbers 11:16–30 shows Moses appointing elders to assist him in administration, and elders are associated with prophets (2 Kings 6:32) and kings (1 Kings 8:1; 20:7, 8; 1 Chronicles 11:3). Every town and city had elders who had roles of authority (1 Kings 21:8, 11; 2 Kings 23:1). In the Gospels and Acts, the "elders of the people" are associated with the chief priests as opponents of Jesus and the early Christians (e.g., Matthew 16:21; 21:23; Acts 4:5–10). It would seem natural that this title would be used by those providing leadership in the early Christian communities.

Peter is not alone in the New Testament in talking about the qualifications needed for those taking the role of elders in Christian communities (Acts 14:22–23; Titus 1:5–6). The fact that elders are appointed presupposes a certain amount of organization in early Christianity. Curiously enough, we find three different approaches to community organization in the New Testament, only one of them featuring elders.[2] For example, in 1 John we find a community divided over issues relating to how Jesus should be understood (1 John 2:18, 19, 26; 4:1–3). Yet the community made no appeal to local church authorities to meet this threat. Instead, in the letters of John there was a strong emphasis on the leadership of the Spirit, which means that "you do not need anyone to teach you" (1 John 2:27, NRSV).

Another type of community organization is envisaged in Matthew 18:15–20, where problems in the community are solved by the whole community gathering together and reaching a communal decision that is going to reflect what would have been decided in heaven.

The third type of Christian community is organized under the leadership of elders. In Acts, for example, we find that Paul either appoints elders to lead Christian communities (Acts 14:22, 23) or finds established communities that already have elders (Acts 20:17; 21:18). These are in addition (or are they the same?—see below) to the deacons, who were found to be necessary to assist the apostles in their work in Acts 6:1–6 and who take on leadership roles within the early groups of believers (Acts 6:8–7:60; 8:4–8, 26–40).

More about the roles of church leaders in early Christianity may be inferred from 1 Timothy 3:1–13 and Titus 1:5–9. Three titles for leaders are found in these verses: elders (Greek *presbuteroi*; Titus 1:5, 6); a bishop (*episkopos*; 1 Timothy 3:1–7; Titus 1:7–9), and deacons (*diakonoi*; 1 Timothy 3:8–13; cf. Philippians 1:1, which mentions deacons and bishops; and Romans 16:1, where Paul mentions Phoebe [a woman] as a deacon). The words used for elders/deacons are always found in the plural form when they are used in the context of leadership positions, implying that a number of them were appointed in each community. Their qualifications are largely related to good moral standing (blameless, married only once, etc., Titus 1:5, 6; serious, not greedy for money, etc., 1 Timothy 3:8–13). The title "bishop" is found in the singular (i.e., there appears to have been only one bishop per Christian community), and a bishop is required to understand sound doctrine and to preach (Titus 1:9). From this it can be inferred that the bishop has a greater responsibility in the community than the elders/deacons.

In the New Testament, the roles accorded to elders and deacons are so similar that it has been suggested that they are two different titles for the same office. If that is the case, then the evidence presented appears to support the conclusion that there were but two types of officials in early Christian communities: a bishop (who had overall responsibility for the community) and a group of elders/deacons (who also played leadership roles). Early in the second century, the three different names had become titles for three different church officers, at least in some regions.[3] At that time, elders and deacons appear to have functioned in a local church, while a bishop had taken on the responsibility for a district of churches.

1 Peter 5:1-5: Three vices to which elders are prone

Peter urges the elders of the Christian communities to which he writes to exercise their leadership role as a shepherd looking after a flock of sheep. The shepherd of the flock is an image found several times in the Bible. For example, God portrays Himself as a patient shepherd gathering His flock in Ezekiel 34:11–16. Jesus also speaks of Himself as a shepherd in John 10:11, a fact acknowledged by Peter, who calls Him the Chief Shepherd (1 Peter 5:4). Likening the role of elders to that of shepherds implies a certain kind of leadership. A shepherd usually allows his flock considerable freedom to forage and rather broad limits to where they can explore. But when it is necessary, he imposes quite strong leadership in the direction the flock ought to move; doing so in a manner that coaxes the sheep rather than punishes them. A shepherd always acts in the best interest of the flock. All qualities, one must admit, that would be admirable in a church leader.

Peter then highlights three vices to which elders are prone. First, some who should lead are reluctant to do so and need to be persuaded to take on leadership roles (verse 2). Such leaders are often halfhearted in their leadership when they take it on. Peter urges them to take on the role with 100 percent commitment.

Second, others take a leadership role as a way to become wealthy (verse 2). Many practices considered normal in the ancient world would be considered to be corrupt in contemporary society. For example, most of those who were appointed governors of Roman provinces were able to enrich themselves by ethically dubious and downright illegal activities. This was also true of lesser functionaries across the Roman Empire, who frequently accepted bribes and other favors. One would not expect too many opportunities to become rich as a leader in the church in the first century, but even so, Peter says that elders should not have this motivation. Third, leadership brings with it a temptation to force others to do what the leader wants them to do (verse 3), rather than through negotiation.

1 Peter 5:3; Matthew 20:24-28: Servant leadership

Peter says that elders should "not lord it over those in your charge." The word *katakurieuontes* in 1 Peter 5:3, translated "being lords over" (KJV), means " 'forcefully ruling over, subduing', and can carry the nuance of a harsh or excessive use of authority (note its use in Mt. 20:25; Mk. 10:42; Acts 19:16; also LXX Gn. 1:28; 9:1; and, in the context of military conquests, Nu. 21:24; 32:22, 29; Ps. 110:2, *etc.*). . . . [Peter] implies that elders should govern not by the use of threats, emotional intimidation, or flaunting of power, but rather by power of example whenever possible."[4]

The words of Peter are reminiscent of those of Jesus, when He says in Matthew 20:25–28, "You know that the rulers of the Gentiles lord it over them, and those who are great exercise authority over them. Yet it shall not be so among you; but whoever desires to become great among you, let him be your servant. And whoever desires to be first among you, let him be your slave—just as the Son of Man did not come to be served, but to serve, and to give His life a ransom for many" (NKJV). Christians have captured the words of Jesus in the concept of "servant leadership." The one who would lead should be the one who serves the most.

1 Peter 5:5-7: Humility

In urging his hearers to clothe themselves with humility (1 Peter 5:5) and to humble themselves before the mighty hand of God (verse 6), Peter is highlighting an attitude that distinguished both Jews and Christians from others in the ancient world. The Roman elite valued and cultivated *gravitas* (seriousness, weight, dignity), *pietas* (duty, loyalty, devotion, religiosity), *dignitas* (dignity, charisma, prestige), and *virtus* (valor, manliness, character, worth), all of which are far removed from humility!

The words used for humility in Greek have a very negative connotation in the Greek-speaking world of the first century and earlier. It indicates a very lowly status. As an adjective it means " 'Lowly,' 'mean,' 'insignificant,' 'weak,' 'poor,' e.g., of the trivial power or significance of a city or country, state or statesman."[5] As a verb, *to humble,* it means " 'to make small or little,' 'to humiliate,' 'to weaken.' "[6] Humility is the attitude that a slave adopts to his or her "betters." This range of meanings, all with negative force, is also found in the Septuagint (the Greek translation of the Old Testament used by early Christians). Yet there is one situation in which humility and abasement are appropriate—that is when humans find themselves in relationship to God.

Humility is a theme in both the Old and New Testaments. The Psalms say, "The LORD lifts up the humble" (Psalm 147:6); "He will beautify the humble with salvation" (Psalm 149:4), and "He does not forget the cry of the humble" (Psalm 9:12). Isaiah 29:19 says that "the humble also shall increase their joy in the LORD," and Proverbs 3:34, "He . . . gives grace to the humble." James 4:10 says, "Humble yourselves in the sight of the Lord, and He will lift you up," and Jesus says, "Whoever humbles himself as this little child is greatest in the kingdom of heaven" (Matthew 18:4).[7]

In both Moses and Jesus, Christians have significant role models who have demonstrated true humility. Moses was said to have been more humble than others (Numbers 12:3). Paul says of Jesus, "And being found in appearance as a man, He humbled Himself and became obedient to the point of death, even the death of the cross" (Philippians 2:8, NKJV).

Peter prefaces his comments about humility by urging the young men in the congregation to be subject to, or subordinate, to the elders—that group that has authority in the Christian community (1 Peter 5:5a). He generalizes this attitude to all within the community. Everybody should be in mutual submission to each other (verse 5b; cf. Philippians 2:3 and Colossians 3:12, where the same word translated "humility," *tapeinophrosunē*, is used). This links the attitude of humility with appropriate worship of God (1 Peter 5:5c, 6, where he uses the more usual words for the noun *humility* and the verb *to be humble*—*tapeinos* and *tapeinoō*).

1 Peter 5:8-10: Like a roaring lion

Peter warns his readers that the devil is prowling around like a lion looking for somebody to devour (verses 8–10). This startling image is given greater force when one considers where a lion seeking to devour people would have been seen by those living in the Roman Empire. Lions were very frequently portrayed in aggressive poses in statues and in mosaics on public buildings, and would have been well known from those sources. But of particular relevance is that lions were one of the beasts of prey used in Roman arenas to "execute" criminals, and many who heard Peter's letter would have seen this horrible sight.[8] This image would have had even greater force in later periods, when Christians were among those torn apart by beasts.[9]

Peter points out that the power of the devil can be seen in the present suffering of his readers. Yet present suffering will end in eternal glory (verse 10). Where there is suffering and temptation, God's grace will restore, support, strengthen, and establish. It is important to know that while the devil is powerful, Jesus is more powerful.

She who is in Babylon

The phrase "She who is in Babylon" in 1 Peter 5:13 (NKJV) is a literal rendition of the original Greek. Most translations correctly capture the meaning of the phrase by translating it as "The *church that is* at Babylon" (KJV, a translation that indicates with italics words that have been added by the translators in rendering the original Greek in intelligible English), or "Your sister church in Babylon" (NRSV). There is near unanimous agreement that by this phrase Peter means the church that is in Rome. His use of the name Babylon invokes the Babylonian exile that dominated much of Old Testament prophetic thought and likens Rome to Babylon, who in the Old Testament was a terrible persecutor and final destroyer of the nation of Judah (e.g., 2 Kings 25:1–26; 2 Chronicles 36:15–23; Isaiah 21:1–10; 47:1–15; Jeremiah 50:1–51:58; Ezekiel 27:1–22; cf. Revelation 18:1–24).[10] Peter begins his letter by addressing it to those who are "exiles of the Dispersion" (1 Peter 1:1, NRSV) and finishes it by using Babylon (1 Peter 5:13) to indicate that the church from which he writes also considered itself to be in "Babylonian" exile while they await the return of Jesus. It is this church, the church at Rome, that sends greetings to those who will receive the letter, along with Mark.

1. William Barclay, *The Letters of James and Peter,* The Daily Study Bible, rev. ed. (Edinburgh, Scotland: Saint Andrew, 1976), 262, 263.

2. See further Robert K. McIver, *The Four Faces of Jesus* (Nampa, ID: Pacific Press®, 2009), 211–216.

3. Early in the second century, Ignatius, third bishop of Antioch in Syria, wrote to a number of churches in Asia Minor. In many of them he urged his hearers to give due obedience to their bishop (e.g., *Ignatius to the Ephesians* 4.1; 5.3; 6.1, 2; *Ignatius to the Magnesians* 3.1, 2; 4.1; 6.1, 2; *Ignatius to the Trallians* 2.1–3; 7.2; 13.2; *Ignatius to the Philadelphians* 4.1; 7.1, 2; 10.2 [which mentions bishops, elders, and deacons]; *Ignatius to the Smyrnaeans* 8:1, 2; 9.1, 2). Commentators have conjectured that Ignatius lays so much stress on the important role of the bishop because their increased authority over church affairs was both recent and contested in some of the churches to which he writes.

4. Grudem, *1 Peter,* 189.

5. Gerhard Kittel, Geoffrey W. Bromiley, and Gerhard Friedrich, eds., *Theological Dictionary of the New Testament* (Grand Rapids, MI: Eerdmans, 1972), VIII, 1.

6. Ibid., 4.

7. All citations in this paragraph are from the NKJV.

8. "Of all the animals known to the Greeks and Romans, lions were probably the most feared, and for that reason they were one of the most anticipated attractions at the Roman games. The sequential order of these spectacles was well known (Seneca, *Ep.* 7.4): animal hunts/fights during the morning,

criminal executions at midday, and gladiatorial contests in the afternoon. Thus, crowds expected the lion to play a major role in the games, and they were rarely disappointed when it did." So say David G. Horrell, Bradley Arnold, and Travis B. Williams, "Visuality, Vivid Description, and the Message of 1 Peter: The Significance of the Roaring Lion (1 Peter 5:8)," *Journal of Biblical Literature* 132 (2013): 708.

9. For example, early in the second century, Ignatius, third bishop of Antioch in Syria, had been condemned to be torn apart by beasts in Rome. He wrote several letters on his way to his martyrdom and urged his followers not to intervene in his behalf. "Suffer me to be eaten by the beasts, through whom I can attain to God." *Ignatius to the Romans* 4.1 (cf. *Ignatius to the Ephesians* 1.2, 3). The citation is taken from *The Apostolic Fathers,* ed. Pope Clement I et al., vol. 1, The Loeb Classical Library (London: Heinemann, 1912), 231. Many Christians were to be executed in this and other manners, up until the time of Constantine, when his patronage of Christianity brought with it a much lesser likelihood that Christians would end up as condemned criminals simply because they were Christians.

10. David Horrell observes, "As most commentators agree, this is almost certainly a reference to Rome, even if it also serves as a symbolic reference to the diasporic situation of the readers." "Between Conformity and Resistance: Beyond the Balch-Elliott Debate Towards a Postcolonial Reading of First Peter," in Webb and Bauman-Martin, *Reading First Peter With New Eyes,* 126.

CHAPTER 8

Jesus in
1 and 2 Peter

Observations about Jesus are found throughout both 1 and 2 Peter. Together they add up to a substantial comment on the special character of Jesus and the importance of His life, death, and resurrection for the whole human race. This chapter will trace the following themes from 1 and 2 Peter: Jesus as our sacrifice; His saving death; His resurrection and glory; and the meaning of the titles Christ, Lord, Savior, and God when applied to Jesus.

Jesus our sacrifice (1 Peter 1:18, 19)

Several phrases in 1 Peter describe the significance of Jesus in terms borrowed from the sacrifices described in the Old Testament. The first of these is found in the second verse of the letter, when he describes the Christians who will hear the letter as those who were destined by God to be obedient to Jesus Christ and to be "sprinkled with his blood" (1 Peter 1:2, NRSV). The phrase "sprinkled with . . . blood" is strongly associated with animal sacrifice, given that the blood to be sprinkled is usually that of the sacrificed animal. In the Old Testament, blood from an animal sacrifice was sprinkled on a number of people and objects. It was sprinkled on Aaron when he was consecrated as the high priest (Exodus 29:19–21); before the curtain between the Holy

Place and Most Holy Place of the temple (Leviticus 4:6, 17); on the side of the altar (Leviticus 5:9); on a cured leper (Leviticus 14:6, 7); on a "leprous" house (verse 51); and on the mercy seat of the ark of the covenant in the Most Holy Place on the Day of Atonement (Leviticus 16:15). The book of Hebrews in the New Testament also notes that both the tent and vessels used in worship were sprinkled with blood (Hebrews 9:21); and blood was sprinkled at the first Passover (Hebrews 11:28). I'm not sure that Peter had any of these instances in mind when he described Christians as sprinkled with the blood of Jesus, but at a minimum, the phrase does tie the death of Jesus with the kind of atonement for sin that was envisaged in the rituals of the temple that was at the heart of the Jewish religion in the first century.

Jesus' death is specifically likened to a sacrifice in 1 Peter 1:18–19, where we are said to be *"redeemed . . . with the precious blood of Christ"* (NIV; emphasis added). But what is meant by the word *redeemed*? The Greek verb *lutroō* used in verse 18 has the basic meaning "to redeem" (as translated by the KJV, NKJV, NIV) or "to release by paying a ransom" (RSV, NRSV).[1] *Redemption* is a word used in the Bible in several ways. For example, the firstborn ass (which could not be sacrificed) and the firstborn son (Exodus 34:19, 20) were redeemed by the sacrifice of a substitute lamb. The redemption/ransom is accepted as the equivalent of the forfeited life—but only because of the graciousness of God.[2] Money could be used to buy back (redeem) items that had been sold because of poverty (Leviticus 25:25, 26). Most important, a slave could be redeemed (Leviticus 25:47–49). First Peter informs readers that the cost of buying them back (redeeming them) from their "futile ways inherited from [their] fathers" (1 Peter 1:18, RSV) was nothing less than the "precious blood of Christ, as of a lamb without blemish" (verse 19, KJV). The language "lamb without blemish" invokes the concept of *animal sacrifice* (cf. the requirement that sacrificial animals be "without blemish" in Leviticus 1:10; 3:1, 6; 4:3, 23, etc.). Several different animals were offered as sacrifices in the Hebrew Bible: bulls and cows, sheep, goats, and turtledoves (Leviticus 3:1, 6, 12; 4:3, 14, 23; 5:7, 11). But when Jesus is portrayed as a sacrifice in the New Testament, it is usually as a lamb (1 Peter 1:19; cf. John 1:29, 36; Acts 8:32–35; Revelation 7:14; 13:8).

In the ritual prescribed in Leviticus, a sheep without blemish was brought by the sinner, who then laid their hands on the animal (Leviticus 4:32, 33). The animal was then slaughtered, and some of its blood was smeared on the altar and the rest poured at the base of the altar (verse 34). In this manner, the death of the sacrificial animal provided "atonement" for the sin of the one who offered the sacrifice (verse 35). By describing the cost of our redemption/ransom as the blood of Jesus and likening Him to a lamb without blemish, 1 Peter 1:18, 19 is saying that Jesus died in our place and His death redeemed us from our sins.

First Peter 1:18, 19 revolves around the double image of redemption and the blood of a sacrifice. Christians have been redeemed at a great cost—the cost of Jesus' death.

Jesus' saving death (1 Peter 2:21-25; 3:18)

The comments about Jesus' suffering in 1 Peter 2:21–25 are found in a context in which Peter is responding to the unjust suffering of Christian house slaves (verses 19, 20). When Peter urges house servants to be patient in their suffering, he is asking nothing more of them than that they should follow the example of Jesus. As Peter says, when Jesus was reviled, He did not revile in return; when He suffered, He did not threaten (verse 23). This language echoes that of Isaiah 53:1–12, a passage used elsewhere by New Testament writers to describe the significance of Jesus' death (e.g., Acts 8:30–35).

There is particular significance to the suffering of Jesus. He "[bore] our sins in his body on the tree [a reference to the cross; cf. Acts 5:30], that we, being dead to sins, should live unto righteousness" (1 Peter 2:24, KJV). Sin brings death (Romans 5:12); and as sinners, we deserve to die. Yet the perfect Jesus—who had no guile on His lips (1 Peter 2:22)—died in our place.

What Peter says next reveals the secret of living as a Christian. Through Jesus' death, we have actually died to sin so that we can live to righteousness (verse 24). Paul uses very similar language in Romans 6:11, when he urges his readers, "Consider yourselves dead to sin and alive to God in Christ Jesus" (RSV). Christians are in the process of making real in their lives what God has already done for them in Jesus. We have died to sin; therefore we should live as though we are dead to sin!

The words of 1 Peter 3:18 return to the theme of Jesus' sacrifice. He, the Righteous One, died for the unrighteous, that He might bring us to God. Jesus died as our substitute, so that we can live a life of righteousness.

Jesus' resurrection and glory (1 Peter 1:3, 4, 21; 3:21, 22; 4:11; 5:4; 2 Peter 1:11)

First Peter is addressed to those who are suffering because of their belief in Jesus (1 Peter 1:6; 3:14; 5:10, etc.). It is particularly appropriate that right at the beginning of his letter, Peter directs his reader's attention to mercy and hope. As he says, the hope of a Christian is a living hope, precisely because it is a hope that rests on the resurrection of Jesus (1 Peter 1:3). Because of Jesus' resurrection, Christians can look forward to an inheritance in heaven that will not perish or fade (verse 4).

Peter's response to the suffering of his Christian readers is therefore twofold. First, he links their suffering to the suffering of Jesus (1 Peter 2:20, 21; 4:12–16). Jesus' suffering is significant because He died in our place so that we might live in righteousness. Second, Jesus' suffering has particular significance because of who He is and because His death was followed by His resurrection.

That Jesus was raised from the dead is a guarantee that we also can be raised (1 Corinthians 15:20, 21). As Paul puts it, "and if Christ be not raised, your faith is vain; ye are yet in your sins" (verse 17, KJV). But because Jesus has been raised from the dead, He has shown He has the power to conquer death itself.

Peter also links the resurrection of Jesus with His glory (1 Peter 1:21). Christian believers will be given a crown of glory at the Second Coming (1 Peter 5:4; cf. 2 Peter 1:11). Peter notes that after His resurrection, Jesus went into the heavens to be at the right hand of God, where the angels and powers were subject to Him (1 Peter 3:22).

Titles of Jesus in 1 and 2 Peter
(Christ, Lord, Savior, Son, and God)

Each of the titles applied to Jesus in 1 and 2 Peter has a rich meaning and conveys an important understanding of His status.

Christ: Jesus is called Jesus Christ no less than fifteen times in 1 and 2 Peter (1 Peter 1:1, 2, 3, 7, 13; 2:5; 3:21; 4:11; 2 Peter 1:1, 8, 11, 14, 16; 2:20; 3:18), and the combination "Jesus Christ" is found in no fewer than 609 verses of the New Testament. The title "Christ" almost functions as part of Jesus' name, although undoubtedly the concept of Messiah was thought of when the name was mentioned. Jesus had been identified as the Christ, or Messiah, during the time of His ministry (e.g., Matthew 16:15, 16), although He discouraged the use of the term, probably because it was widely misunderstood (verse 20; Mark 8:29). To Jesus, the Messiah was one who suffered. For example, when Peter correctly identified Jesus as the Christ, Jesus immediately begins to talk of His coming suffering (Matthew 16:16, 21–23).

Lord: The title *Lord* is used six times in 1 Peter (1:3, 25; 2:3; 3:6, 12, 15) and fourteen times in 2 Peter (1:2, 8, 11, 14, 16; 2:9, 11, 20; 3:2, 8, 9, 10, 15, 18). Within the wider New Testament, the title "lord" can have a purely secular meaning. It is how you would address a social superior such as a king or landowner (e.g., Matthew 25:44; Luke 13:8; 14:21–23). It can be used as a title of respect, rather like the word *sir* in English. Another use in the New Testament relates to God. For example, in the phrases "Lord God" or "the Lord our God," *Lord* is a title ascribed to God Himself (e.g., Mark 12:29; Luke 1:16, 32). In fact, *The Lord* or *Lord* can be a term meaning God (e.g., Luke 1:9; 20:37; Acts 2:25; 7:33; Romans 11:2, 3).

Peter uses *Lord* in the secular sense of "sir" (1 Peter 3:6) and for God the Father (e.g., 1 Peter 1:25). Mostly, though, it is a term attached to Jesus, as in the phrases "Lord Jesus Christ" (1 Peter 1:3; 2 Peter 1:8, 14, 16) and "Lord and Savior Jesus Christ" (2 Peter 2:20; 3:18). In 1 and 2 Peter, as in the other letters of the New Testament, the title *Lord* has considerable overtones of divinity.

Savior: In the Hebrew Bible, a "savior" is one who rescues people, usually from captivity (e.g., Judges 3:9, 15; Isaiah 19:20). God Himself could take on this role (Psalm 106:21; Isaiah 43:3). Within the New Testament, Jesus is the one who will save the world from sin (John 4:42; cf. 1 Timothy 1:15). The word *savior* is used five times in 2 Peter (1:1, 11; 2:20; 3:2, 18). Each time it is a reference to Jesus, four times as "Lord and Savior," and three of those as "Lord and Savior Jesus Christ."

God: Like other writers in the New Testament, Peter describes the relationship between Jesus and God with the words *Father* and *Son*. For example, "Blessed be the God and Father of our Lord Jesus Christ" (1 Peter 1:3, KJV; cf. 2 Peter 1:17). Jesus is described as the loved Son (2 Peter 1:17), and some of Jesus' authority as Lord and His heavenly status come from this special relationship that He has with God the Father. Yet Peter also describes Jesus as "God"; 2 Peter 1:1 mentions "our God and Savior Jesus Christ." In the Greek original, the same definite article (i.e., "the") is used for both God and Savior. Grammatically this means that both "God" and "Savior" are used of Jesus.[3] Second Peter 1:1, then, stands as one of the very clear indications of the full divinity of Jesus in the New Testament (see also John 1:1; 20:28).

As the early Christians struggled to understand Jesus, they gradually put the evidence of the New Testament together. The Father, the Son, and the Holy Spirit are distinct in 1 Peter (e.g., Father/Son, 1 Peter 1:3; 2 Peter 1:17; Holy Spirit, 1 Peter 1:12; 2 Peter 1:21), as indeed they are in the rest of the New Testament. Yet at the same time, Jesus is portrayed as fully divine, as is the Holy Spirit. Over time, and after much discussion, the church developed the doctrine of the Trinity to explain as best as possible the divine mystery of the Godhead.[4]

---

1. In classical Greek usage, the Septuagint (LXX), and usage contemporary to the New Testament, the verb *lutroō* has the basic meaning of "to free by ransom." As observed in Gerhard Kittel, Geoffrey W. Bromiley, and Gerhard Friedrich, eds., *Theological Dictionary of the New Testament* (Grand Rapids, MI: Eerdmans, 1967), 4:349, 350, "In the NT we find only the med. λυτροῦσθαι, and it is used exclusively for the redeeming act of God or of Jesus. The usage seems to be the same as that of the LXX. The only point is

how far it carries with it the idea of a ransom."

2. "The Jewish view is the same as the general view of antiquity. 'Ransom money (*purkan*) . . . is . . . an equivalent for forfeited life. In Rabb. law the ref. is to death decreed by God, from which there is release by ransom. . . . It is significant that the acceptance and amount of the ransom are dependent on the good will of the one to whom it is offered.' " *Theological Dictionary of the New Testament,* 4:341. The reference provided for words quoted is "Dalman, 110."

3. This grammatical feature is known as the Granville Sharp rule. See further examples in McIver, *Intermediate New Testament Greek Made Easier,* 199, 200; and for a comprehensive treatment and a copious set of examples, see Wallace, *Greek Grammar: Beyond the Basics,* 270–290.

4. Kelly, *Early Christian Doctrines,* 83–162, 223–343 provides a very helpful overview of the development of the doctrine of the trinity, along with many of the ideas explored and rejected as satisfactory along the way. For an exploration of the biblical, historical, and theological evidence that make up the modern understanding of trinity, see also the papers in Paul Petersen and Rob McIver, eds., *Biblical and Theological Studies on the Trinity* (Adelaide/ Cooranbong, Australia: ATF/Avondale Academic Press, 2014); and Woodrow Whidden, Jerry Moon, John W. Reeve, *The Trinity* (Hagerstown, MD: Review and Herald®, 2002).

CHAPTER 9

Making One's Calling and Election Sure

2 Peter 1:1-15

Second Peter addresses a slightly different set of concerns than those found in 1 Peter. Suffering dominates 1 Peter but is virtually absent in 2 Peter (e.g., the verb "to suffer" occurs eleven times in 1 Peter but is absent from 2 Peter; 2 Peter 2:9 is the one mention of the godly experiencing a "trial"). The greatest threat to believers in 2 Peter is not suffering for their faith, but false teachers (e.g., 2 Peter 2:1–3:7).

Like 1 Peter, 2 Peter uses long sentences made up of shorter ideas linked together. Understanding what he says, then, grows out of identifying and understanding each of these smaller units, and noticing how they are linked together to make the wider point that Peter wishes to make. And his point is profound: Christians need to make real in their lives what they already are in Christ.

2 Peter 1:1-4: Partakers in the divine nature

Second Peter 1:1, like 1 Peter 1:1, begins as a standard letter. It identifies the author (Peter) and the recipients, although the terms used to describe who should receive the letter are somewhat vague. Who does Peter mean when he says, "to them that have obtained like precious faith with us" (verse 1, KJV; or "a faith of equal standing with ours," RSV)? The word Peter uses that is translated as "precious/equal standing" means "of equal value" or "of equal privilege." Why would he compare their value or privilege with "us"? Does he mean the twelve disciples of Jesus; or does he mean "us, who are Christians of Jewish heritage"?

Most likely, the use of the word "dispersion/strangers" in 1 Peter 1:1 indicates that 1 Peter was sent to Christians who were largely of Jewish heritage. So a case could be made here that this second letter was addressed to Gentile Christians. The fact that Peter had a particular group in mind is clear from the way he addresses specific issues among those he is writing to and his declaration of having sent them a previous letter (2 Peter 3:1).

Within the thirty-five words that form the first two verses of 1 Peter in the Greek New Testament, Peter mentions Jesus three times, and God is twice in conjunction with Jesus ("Jesus Christ," "God and Savior Jesus Christ," and "God and Jesus our Lord"; fifteen words). "By this repetition, Peter foregrounds Jesus and God as the central figures for the argument that follows."[1]

The words in 2 Peter 1:3, 4 are connected grammatically to 2 Peter 1:2 (1 Peter 1:1–4 is one sentence[2]). This means that verses 3 and 4 are about the same topic as 2 Peter 1:2—knowledge of God and Jesus our Lord.

Peter emphasizes that the divine power of Jesus has given to us everything that concerns life and godliness (2 Peter 1:3). Believers have been given two precious and great promises: (1) they will escape corruption by the suitable control of passion (verse 4); and (2) they will partake in the divine nature (verse 4). These things are provided through knowledge of Jesus (verse 3). This is not necessarily a knowledge that comes from study—although that can be helpful. Rather, it is a knowledge that comes because Jesus has called us. He has revealed to us His glory and excellence (verse 3).

2 Peter 1:5-7: Love, the goal of Christian virtue

There are several lists of virtues in the New Testament (e.g., Matthew 5:2–12; 2 Corinthians 6:6, 7; Ephesians 6:14–17; Philippians 4:8; Colossians 3:12–16; 1 Timothy 3:2, 3; 6:11; Titus 1:7–8; 2 Peter 1:5–8), as well as lists of vices (e.g., Mark 7:21, 22;

Romans 1:29, 30; 1 Corinthians 5:10; 6:9, 10; Ephesians 5:3–5; Colossians 3:5, 8; 1 Timothy 1:9, 10; 6:4, 5; 2 Timothy 3:2–5; Jude 8, 16; Revelation 9:20, 21), and some lists that combine virtues and vices (Luke 6:20–26; Galatians 5:16–23; Ephesians 4:31, 32; James 3:15–17).[3] The lists appear to have been composed to fit the context of the writing and with an eye to rhythm and alliteration.

Second Peter 1:5–7 is a little different from the other lists found in the New Testament, in that each virtue builds on the previous virtue (although Paul uses the device of one good thing building on another in Romans 10:14, 15; and 8:29, 30). For Peter, the virtues begin with faith and end with love.

Each of the virtues Peter uses has significant meaning:

- Faith: Faith is nothing less than a saving belief in Jesus; although in lists of virtues it might also convey the meaning of faithfulness in fulfilling duties.
- Virtue: Virtue is a standard item in lists of virtues given by Greek philosophers, although, interestingly enough, in the New Testament only Peter includes it in his list.
- Knowledge: Knowledge is being well informed. Peter has already highlighted knowledge in the previous verses. Here he is probably particularly thinking about knowledge of God's saving acts in Jesus.
- Temperance/self-control: The word translated "self-control" (*enkrateian*) means lordship or control. In the context of a list of virtues, it means control over self. The concept played an important role in the ethics of Greek philosophers. "In view of all this, it is striking how small a part is played by the term in biblical religion."[4]
- Patience/steadfastness: In Greek classical literature, the word translated as "steadfastness," *hupomonē,* had the concept of bravely standing firm against external threat. In the Greek translation of the Old Testament used by early Christians (the Septuagint), the word took on the concept of waiting patiently for God in hope. For example, it is translated as "hope" in 1 Chronicles 29:15;

Jeremiah 14:8 (NIV). In the New Testament it is used to describe the steadfastness of Christ (2 Thessalonians 3:5). In Revelation 3:10 it explains the patient endurance of those Christians who have been persecuted.

- Godliness: The Greek word translated "godliness" (*eusebeia*) in 2 Peter 1:6, 7 is also found in 3:11 (and Acts 10:2, 7; and several times in 1 Timothy—e.g., 2:2; 3:16, etc.). "It denotes piety towards the gods, but also, especially in Jewish and Christian usage, the respect for God's will and the moral way of life which are inseparable from proper religious attitude to God."[5]
- Brotherly kindness/brotherly love: Christians are like a family, and godliness will lead to a community that loves each other like a family.
- Love/charity:[6] Although godliness is one of the important virtues and comes toward the end of Peter's list, the pinnacle virtue for a Christian is not godliness, but love!

2 Peter 1:8-11: Be what you are

Second Peter 2:8–11 touches on matters that go to the heart of the Christian experience. These verses raise the issue of the real difference that being a Christian should make in the life of a believer. Peter has just listed the progression in Christian virtue that starts with faith and ends with love. He then makes the following points about these virtues:

- These things are already "yours" (plural) and "increasing among you" (plural) (verse 8a, NRSV)—Peter uses the plural because he is thinking about the Christian community as a whole.
- Anyone lacking these virtues is forgetful of the cleansing from previous sins (verse 9).
- Therefore, Christians should make sure for themselves their election and calling—presumably by exhibiting these virtues in their lives (verse 10). If they do so, they will "never stumble" (NRSV).

In saying these things, Peter highlights that there is a component of human activity in salvation. Indeed, one way to read the reference to making our election sure is to understand that Peter is insisting that Christian actions may contribute to their salvation.[7] Peter knows the letters of Paul (2 Peter 3:15, 16), but has he misunderstood their emphasis that humans are saved by faith, as a gift of God and quite apart from works of law (Galatians 2:16; Ephesians 2:8)? No, not when you consider his words carefully. After all, Peter insists that the virtues *start* with faith (1 Peter 1:5)—it is from there that all other Christian virtues follow. Peter insists that Christians who do not show Christian virtues have misunderstood (2 Peter 1:8) and forgotten (verse 9) the reality of their salvation. In fact, Peter has already stated in verse 3 that "His divine power has given us everything needed for life and godliness, through the knowledge of him who called us by his own glory and goodness" (NRSV). Christians have been cleansed from past sins (verse 9; through baptism); they *have* been given salvation. What Christians do is build on their initial faith. They do indeed confirm their election by what they do, but it is something they confirm for themselves not for God. They are not seeking to be saved by what they do, but they are making real in their own lives what is already true in Jesus.[8]

Second Peter 1:8–11 captures something that is said elsewhere in the New Testament by Paul. Note how in one place he describes what is real for Christians, and in another he urges them to act on the new reality. For example, in Galatians 5:24 Paul says that in Christ we have already crucified the flesh, but in Romans 8:13 we are told to put to death the deeds of the body. According to Romans 6:18, we are slaves of righteousness, but in Romans 6:13 we are told to present our members as instruments of righteousness. Paul says Christians are already transformed in 2 Corinthians 3:18; 4:16, 17, but in Romans 12:2 we are called to be transformed. In Romans 6:5–10 Paul says that in baptism we join in the death of Christ and die to sin, but in Romans 6:11 he urges us consider ourselves dead to sin. We are to live in the light of the new reality that Jesus' death and resurrection has brought about.

Both Peter and Paul say, "You are—therefore be!" Be all that is already true for you in Jesus!

2 Peter 1:12-15: Putting off the body?

Peter speaks of his impending death in 2 Peter 1:14, leading many commentators to consider that 2 Peter belongs to two literary genres at the same time: the letter and the farewell speech.[9] The last words of important leaders are often taken with great seriousness, as for example, the last words of Isaac (Genesis 27:1–40) and Jacob (Genesis 48:1–49:27). So 2 Peter is written by someone who is very conscious that he does not have much longer to live and considers what he has to say very important. As Peter says, "And I will make every effort so that after my departure you may be able at any time to recall these things" (2 Peter 1:15); while 2 Peter is a letter, true, it is also a last testament.

Peter uses a colloquial idiom to express his impending death, one that is caught well by the King James Version, which translates it as "shortly I must put off this my tabernacle" (verse 14). Peter likens his body to a "tent," which, when he takes it off as he would a garment, signals that he has died. While he uses a slightly different word (*skēnos* rather than *skēnōmatos*; the words are very similar in meaning), Paul uses similar imagery to foreshadow his own death in 2 Corinthians 5:1–5. He, too, likens death to putting off his body rather like having a tent that he is living in destroyed (verse 1), or taking it off (verse 3). It is possible to read these images as implying that toward the end of their life, both Peter and Paul were thinking in terms of their souls surviving the destruction of their body. Yet this is unlikely for a number of reasons. The New Testament is consistent in viewing the future hope of Christians after they die in terms of resurrection. For example, when Paul speaks of death, he does not speak of immortality but of resurrection (1 Thessalonians 4:13–18; 1 Corinthians 15:12–56). Interestingly enough, Jesus also does the same thing (John 11:1–44). He talks of death as a sleep from which we must be awoken in the resurrection (verses 11, 13). When the New Testament talks about death, it does so in terms of resurrection, not immortality of the soul.[10]

In the Hebrew Bible it was the combination of spirit/breath and body that made up a human being. Genesis 2:7 reads, "And the LORD God formed man of the dust of the ground, and breathed into his nostrils the breath of life; and man became a living soul" (KJV), or "living being" (NRSV). God created the first human by first making a body, and then breathing into it the breath of life. Both body and spirit were required for human life to exist. Without one or the other, life ceases. As Ecclesiastes 12:7 says, at death, "then shall the dust return to the earth as it was: and the spirit shall return unto God who gave it" (KJV). Within the New Testament also there is no conception of a future life after death without the involvement of a body. Believers who have died will be resurrected, but they are resurrected with a body. Without a body they have no existence.

So what do we make of Peter and Paul's description of their impending death as putting off the tent of their body? It is likely just a colloquialism, such as we would say in English, "shuffling off this mortal coil." Though I have no real idea what that means, I like the sound of it and use it when speaking of death in a wry manner. Often phrases have taken on a new meaning beyond its original meaning, and Peter and Paul most likely meant nothing more than they were conscious that their lives were coming to an end. This is, no doubt, why the phrase in 2 Peter 1:14, translated as "shortly I must put off this my tabernacle" in the King James Version, is translated as "I know that my death will come soon" in the New Revised Standard Version.

---

1. James C. Miller, "The Sociological Category of 'Collective Identity' and Its Implications for Understanding Second Peter," in Robert L. Webb and Duane F. Watson, eds., *Reading Second Peter with New Eyes: Methodological Reassessments of the Letter of Second Peter* (London: T&T Clark, 2010), 162.

2. Grant R. Osborne agrees that "in Greek, 1:1–4 is a single sentence." Osborne and Mulholland, *James, 1–2 Peter, Jude, Revelation*, 288.

3. These lists are all discussed in Burton Scott Easton, "New Testament Ethical Lists," *Journal of Biblical Literature* 51 (1932): 1–12. See also the analysis of the list of virtues in 2 Peter 1:5–7 in Richard Bauckham, *Jude–2 Peter*, 174–188.

4. Kittel, Bromiley, Friedrich, *Theological Dictionary of the New Testament*, 341.

5. Bauckham, *Jude–2 Peter*, 178.

6. If nothing else, the fact that the King James Version uses the word *charity* to translate the Greek word *agapē* here and in 1 Corinthians 13 shows how the English language has changed since the time of King James. Any modern translation would translate the word *agapē* as "love," and such is its true meaning.

7. This possibility is considered, and rejected, by Douglas J. Moo, who considers it in the context of a debate common among Baptists between Calvinists (who emphasize the divine election of God, apart from human works) and Arminians (who emphasize the importance of what believers do). See *The NIV Application Commentary: 2 Peter, Jude* (Grand Rapids, MI: Eerdmans, 1996), 58–60.

8. "Peter does not insert works as something necessary for Christians to achieve salvation. The Christians' act of confirming does not save them from their sins. From God's perspective, no confirmation is needed. Rather, the Christians' demonstration of such virtues in their lives confirms for themselves (note the middle voice of ποιεῖσθαι) and for their neighbors that they are called and elected by Christ. Such virtues as those listed in 2 Pet 1:5–7 demonstrate the existence of true faith." Curtis P. Giese, *2 Peter and Jude*, Concordia Commentary (St. Louis, MO: Concordia, 2012), 59.

9. See the extensive notes in Bauckham, *Jude–2 Peter*, 131–135. Cf.: "Following Bauckham, we can see the importance of the impending death of Peter (2 Pet 1:12–15) as that which binds together the whole letter." Richard B. Vinson, Richard F. Wilson, and Watson E. Mills, *1 & 2 Peter, Jude* (Macon, GA: Smyth & Helwys, 2010), 274. As Bauckham points out (p. 131), "In the intertestamental period there was a considerable vogue for accounts of the last words of OT heroes, whether as independent works (e.g. *T. Moses.*, *T.12 Patr.*, *T. Job*, *1 Enoch 91–104*) or as parts of historical or pseudo-historical works (e.g. Tob 14:3–11; 4 Ezra 14:28–36; *2 Apoc. Bar.* 57–86; *Jub.* 21–22; 35; 36:1–18; *Bib. Ant.* 19:1–5; 24:1–5; 28:3–4, 5–10; 33; *Adam and Eve* 25–29; Josephus, *Ant.* 4.309–19). Such testaments had two main types of content: (1) Ethical Admonition . . . (2) Revelations of the future."

10. In the foreword of his 1958 English translation of a short study first published in 1956, Oscar Cullmann notes, "No other publication of mine has provoked such enthusiasm or such violent hostility." His study was called *Immortality of the Soul or Resurrection of the Dead? The Witness of the New Testament* (London: Epworth, 1958). In it he pointed out that the concept of the resurrection is quite incompatible with the concept of the immortal soul. Furthermore, he argues that the New Testament lies squarely on the side of the resurrection of the dead. The work that convinced most New Testament scholars of the correctness of this general position was that of Rudolf Bultmann, *Theologie des Neuen Testaments* (Tübingen, Germany: Mohr, 1953), 189–249 (English translation: *Theology of the New Testament*, 2 vols. [London: SCM, 1952, 1955]). By a careful exposition of the Greek text of Paul's writings, Bultmann demonstrated that the terms *body*, *soul*, and *spirit* are just

different ways of looking at humans in their entirety. For example, "Man does not have a *soma* [body], he *is* a body, for in not a few cases *soma* can be translated 'I' . . . thus, 1 Cor. 13:3; 9:27; 7:4" (1:194). "Paul uses *psyche* [soul] altogether in the sense current in the Old Testament-Jewish tradition; viz. to designate human life, or rather to denote man as a living being" (1:204). See also Robert Jewett, *Paul's Anthropological Terms* (Leiden, Netherlands: E. J. Brill, 1971); W. G. Kümmel, *Das Bild des Menschen im Neuen Testament* (Zürich, Switzerland: Zwingli, 1948) (English translation: *Man in the New Testament* [London: Epworth, 1963]); and (for a synthesis of much of the foregoing set out in an easy-to-understand manner) George Eldon Ladd, *A Theology of the New Testament* (Grand Rapids, MI: Eerdmans, 1974), 457–478.

Prophecy and Scripture
1 Peter 1:10-12; 2 Peter 1:16-20

The Bible plays a very helpful role in the life of a Christian when it comes to difficult moral decisions: it reveals God's dealings with humanity; it provides examples of those who have or have not made good decisions with their lives; and it provides guidance on the principles by which we should live. As Peter says, it can be like "a lamp shining in a dark place" (2 Peter 1:19, NRSV). In his letters, Peter also comments on the role of prophets (1 Peter 1:10–12), and that of eyewitnesses and the more sure word of prophecy (2 Peter 1:16–20). In passing he also reveals two important principles by which he interprets Scripture.

1 Peter 1:10-12: The prophets' search for salvation

In 1 Peter 1:10–12, Peter points out to his readers that their knowledge of salvation is far superior to that of the prophets of old. It is striking that Peter observes that not only were the prophets the recipients of special revelation from God, but they also made careful search and inquiry about the meaning of those revelations. Spiritual insight, then, is given to those who seek understanding and who study the Scriptures.

Peter notes that the messages given to the prophets were given by the "Spirit of Christ" (verse 11). Paul also uses this expression, in Philippians 1:19; a similar expression, the "Spirit of God," in

Romans 8:9 and Philippians 3:3; the "Spirit of life in Christ" in Romans 8:2; and a related expression, "Spirit of Holiness," in Romans 1:4. That Peter and Paul use these expressions to refer to the Holy Spirit is clear (compare "Spirit of Christ" in 1 Peter 1:11 with "Holy Spirit" in verse 12). But the fact that Peter says it was the "Spirit of Christ" who inspired the prophets of old is significant. It is nothing less than a statement that Christ has been active throughout all time in revealing His salvation to His people.

The Spirit of Christ revealed two things to the prophets of old: the sufferings of Christ and the subsequent glory (verse 11). These two strands can be found throughout the Hebrew Bible. The sufferings of the Messiah can be seen in the following passages: Genesis 3:15; Psalm 22; Isaiah 52:13–53:12; Zechariah 12:10; 13:7. His glory, from the following passages: Psalm 110; Isaiah 53:12; Jeremiah 33:14, 15; Daniel 7:13, 14.

Peter assures his readers that they occupy a very special place in history. To them has been revealed in full what had only been partially revealed to the prophets. The prophets indeed spoke to their own times, but crucial parts of their message would not be fulfilled until the coming of the Christ. Jesus would be the One who would bring healing and salvation. He would be the One who would be given glory by God.

The good news is "now reported unto you by them that have preached the gospel unto you with the Holy Ghost sent down from heaven" (1 Peter 1:12, KJV). Peter outlines the several avenues of communication by which God has communicated His message to Peter's readers. First, the Spirit of Christ revealed it to the prophets. Second, it has been preached. Third, the Holy Ghost (KJV)/Holy Spirit (NRSV) is working on the hearts of the believers.

2 Peter 1:16-18: Eyewitnesses of majesty

In 2 Peter 1:12–15, Peter points out the particular solemnity of the occasion on which he writes: he expects to die soon. His words, then, are a kind of "last will and testament." His next words, found in verses 16 through 18, share his most important insight: Christianity is grounded in a reality of which he is an eyewitness. As Peter says, Christianity is not founded on "cunningly devised fables" (verse 16, KJV) but on real events that happened in history. This is true. We know where Jesus was born (Bethlehem; Matthew 2:1–11; Luke 2:1–7), where He grew up (Nazareth; Matthew 2:19–23; Luke 2:29–40), His profession (carpenter; Mark 6:3), the names of His mother and brothers (Mary, James, Joses and Judas; He also had sisters; Mark 6:3). The stories that are told about Him take place in real towns and cities (Nazareth, Capernaum, Jerusalem), and the government officials that handle His trial are known from historical sources (Pilate, Herod; Matthew 27:2; Mark 15:1; Luke 23:1, 7).

Peter explains that he is an eyewitness, and indeed the names of many of the eyewitnesses of Jesus' life, death, and resurrection are known even today: Matthew, John, Peter, and James have all left written documents. We also know of Mary the mother of Jesus, and Mary Magdalene, Martha, Luke, and Mark as well as a long list of others who were eyewitnesses to crucial moments in the ministry of Jesus. Even Paul has a claim to be an eyewitness, in that he met the risen Jesus (1 Corinthians 15:3–9). Peter and the other eyewitnesses are the faithful witnesses of what they heard Jesus say and watched Him do.

Peter highlights one incident of which he was an eyewitness: the transfiguration of Jesus (2 Peter 1:17, 18). This account, found in Matthew 17:1–8; Mark 9:2–8, and Luke 9:28–36, contains all the elements that Peter mentions in 2 Peter 1:17, 18: Peter (along with James and John) was with Jesus on the holy mountain (verse 18; cf. Mark 9:2); and they heard the voice say, "This is my Son, my Beloved, with whom I am well pleased" (2 Peter 1:17, NRSV; cf. Mark 9:7).

Peter was an eyewitness to the ministry of Jesus, including the extraordinary moment when Jesus was revealed in glory on the Mount of Transfiguration. He says his experiences have made the words of the prophets more certain, or completely certain.[1] He does not specify which prophetic words he is thinking about, but because he has just been speaking about witnessing the life of Jesus, and will return to the centrality of Jesus in the next few lines, it would appear likely that Peter would be thinking about those prophecies that point to a coming Savior and that find their fulfillment in Jesus.

How to understand the Bible (1 Peter 1:10-12; 2 Peter 1:20)

Peter observes that the prophets of old made careful search and inquiry as to the meaning of the prophecies they were given. If the prophets who were so spiritually blessed searched the Scriptures, how much more should we seek to understand Scripture aright? But how are we to go about doing that? Modern writers answering this question would no doubt mention the importance of taking account of the historic and cultural backgrounds of a biblical text and would consider the difference between what the text meant to its original hearers and what it means in today's society.[2] We don't know how Peter would have answered this question, because he only addresses it obliquely. What he does do is provide two important principles that he thinks should guide how the Bible is interpreted. Scriptures are not of private interpretation (2 Peter 1:20), and the whole of Scripture witnesses to Jesus (1 Peter 1:10–12). So for Peter, Scripture is something that is understood in the community of faith. As groups study Scripture, the Spirit will lead them into an understanding that is common to them all. Peter also insists that Jesus is the heart of the revelation of God. In Jesus, all the promises of God come true, and in Jesus, the hope of all Christians will be realized. Jesus, in fact, is both the content and the context to be considered when interpreting Scripture.

---

1. Peter Davids notes, "In our verse the comparative is used, so we are not talking about making something certain or reliable, but more certain/more reliable. Given that in Koine Greek the comparative was frequently used as if it were a superlative, the meaning could also be 'most certain /reliable' or 'completely certain.' " *The Letters of 2 Peter and Jude,* Pillar New Testament Commentary (Grand Rapids, MI: Eerdmans, 2006), 207.

2. See "Methods of Bible Study: Action Voted at the 1986 Annual Council," *Ministry* 60 (April 1987): 22–24. See further Robert K. McIver, "Bible Alive: How to Understand the 'Plain Meaning' of the Bible," *Adventist*

Review, August 13, 1992, 8–10 [864–866]; Robert K. McIver and Ray C. W. Roennfeldt, "Text and Interpretation: Christian Understandings of Authoritative Texts in the Light of Social Change," *Islam and Christian-Muslim Relations* 20 (2009): 257–276.

False Teachers

2 Peter 2:1-3:7

There are few who have not been the unwitting listener to a phone conversation of a stranger on public transportation or in a restaurant. You can tell quite a lot about the person at the other end of the phone and their relationship by what you hear. It is easy enough to tell if the phone call is from a boy to his girl-friend; or from a girl to a female friend; or from a salesperson to a potential customer. If there is a difference of opinion, it is often possible to put together the clues to get a reasonable idea of what the issue is just from the one part of the conversation that is overheard.

Reading 2 Peter is a little like listening to a mobile phone conversation. We are only hearing half the dialogue. We can understand that there is a problem—false teachers. We can even make out some of the issues that are being raised by the false teachers. Yet there are intriguing gaps known only to Peter and his recipients. We will understand 2 Peter much better if we can work out the issue that Peter is addressing, and this chapter will attempt just that.

What do the false teachers teach? (2 Peter 2:1-3, 10-22; 3:1-7)

Second Peter 2:1 most likely reveals the reason Peter felt the need to write the letter—there were false teachers active in the churches. Furthermore, because he describes these false teachers as being "among you" (verse 1), they must claim to be Christians, and they have been successful in attracting followers (verses 3, 19).

Peter outlines the following characteristics of the false teachers and what they are saying:

- Their teaching results in licentiousness (verses 2, 3). The Greek word used in verse 2, *aselgeia*, means "sensuality, indecency, vice" and is translated as "pernicious" in the KJV, "shameful" in the NIV, and "licentious" in the NRSV.
- They are not afraid to revile or blaspheme the glorious ones (verses 10, 11).
- They count it a pleasure to revel in the daytime and have eyes full of adultery and hearts trained in greed (verses 13, 14).
- They entice with licentious passions of the flesh, getting believers to return to the very behavior of their previous life they had left behind when they became Christians (verses 18–22).
- They promise freedom or liberty but are actually ensnared in corruption (verse 19).

The other explicit clues that Peter provides about the beliefs and practices of the false teachers are found in 2 Peter 3:3–7. He notes that scoffers will arise, asking, "Where is the promise of his coming?" Given Peter's reaction (e.g., verses 8–10), it is clear that these scoffers were already in existence. It is also highly likely that they are the very same false teachers referred to in chapter 2. We can see, then, the reasoning that allows the false teachers to suggest immorality and licentious behavior is appropriate to Christians. They claim that Jesus will not, in fact, return, and therefore the last judgment will not happen. It means that there will be no future accountability for their behavior.

These, then, are the explicit things that Peter says about the false teachers. But there may be other clues in the letter about what the false teachers are teaching.

For example, why would Peter feel the need to warn against misreading Paul in 2 Peter 3:15, 16? Are the false teachers reading Paul in a way that leads to "lawlessness" (verse 17)? Or why does Peter insist that Christians have not followed cunningly devised fables (2 Peter 1:16)? Is it because the false teachers have accused Peter and the other disciples of making up some things about Jesus? Or is he saying that the false teachers follow cunningly devised fables?

Putting all this together, we find that Peter is very concerned about a group of false teachers who deny that Jesus will return. These teachers are leading some Christians into sinful behavior much like what they had previously put behind them. Peter thinks they are in great danger of facing God's punishing judgment when Jesus returns.

2 Peter and Jude: Judgments against angels, Noah's generation, Sodom and Gomorrah, Lot, and Balaam

It is the outcome of bad behavior that is at the heart of Peter's concern about the teachings taught by the false teachers (2 Peter 2:1–3, 18–22). It is also the reason he gives such a strong warning against such teachings. Because of this, Peter gives a series of examples when God has intervened in human history to punish this kind of behavior. He cites the judgements that have fallen on the angels who sinned (verse 4), Noah's generation (verse 5), Sodom and Gomorrah (verse 6), and Balaam (verse 15). This set of judgments is quite similar to those recounted by Jude. He speaks of the angels who did not keep their own position and are being kept in eternal chains (Jude 6), Sodom and Gomorrah (verse 7), and Balaam (verse 11).

The relationship between 2 Peter and Jude is widely recognized, and worth exploring here a little, because the source of some of the ideas of Jude is made clear in Jude 14; and if there is a strong connection between 2 Peter and Jude, Jude 14 may reveal a background for some of the ideas in 2 Peter. There are many parallels between 2 Peter 2:1–3:4 and Jude 4–19, some of which are listed in the table below.[1] The texts are taken from the New International Version.

2 Peter 2	Jude
1 . . . just as there will be false teachers among you. They will secretly introduce destructive heresies, even denying the sovereign Lord who bought them—bringing swift destruction on themselves.	4 For certain individuals . . . have secretly slipped in among you. They are ungodly people, who pervert the grace of our God into a license for immorality and deny Jesus Christ our only Sovereign and Lord.
4 For if God did not spare angels when they sinned, but sent them to hell, putting them in chains of darkness to be held for judgment . . .	6 And the angels who did not keep their positions of authority but abandoned their proper dwelling—these he has kept in darkness, bound with everlasting chains for judgment on the great Day.
6 if he condemned the cities of Sodom and Gomorrah by burning them to ashes, and made them an example of what is going to happen to the ungodly . . .	7 In a similar way, Sodom and Gomorrah and the surrounding towns gave themselves up to sexual immorality and perversion. They serve as an example of those who suffer the punishment of eternal fire.
10–12	8–10
15 They have left the straight way and wandered off to follow the way of Balaam son of Bezer, who loved the wages of wickedness.	11 Woe to them! They have taken the way of Cain; they have rushed for profit into Balaam's error; they have been destroyed in Korah's rebellion.
3:3 Above all, you must understand that in the last days scoffers will come, scoffing and following their own evil desires.	17 But, dear friends, remember what the apostles of our Lord Jesus Christ foretold. 18 They said to you, "In the last times there will be scoffers who will follow their own ungodly desires."

Commentators invariably discuss the relationship between 2 Peter and Jude (in fact, most commentaries on 2 Peter also include a commentary on Jude). They usually conclude that Peter knew the book of Jude and uses it as a source of ideas and phrases,[2] and at least one writer has tried to argue that Peter is doing what other ancient writers did: imitate the work of Jude, which he admired.[3] I think it likely that Peter knew the book of Jude, and used his flow of thought. But that is secondary to the way this illuminates what Peter says about the casting into hell of the angels who sinned, which is found in 2 Peter 2:4.

2 Peter 2:4-6: Judgments against the angels, the generation of Noah, and Sodom

In 2 Peter 2:1–3, Peter has warned against the dangers of the false teachers—their teachings will lead to licentious ways. He then shows the danger of such behavior. It is exactly the type of behavior that will incur the wrath of God. Peter then cites several examples of the link between licentious behavior and the judgement of God.

The first example he gives is that of the angels of heaven who had sinned and been cast into hell[4] (2 Peter 2:4). We read about angels who sinned in the pictorial language of Revelation 12:7–9, which is one possible background to 2 Peter 2:4, although a more likely background is to be found in 1 Enoch. This work is cited directly by Jude 14 and appears to be the background of the "angels . . . kept in eternal chains" in Jude 6.

First Enoch returns several times to the implications of Genesis 6:1, 2, which states, "When people began to multiply on the face of the ground, and daughters were born to them, the sons of God saw that they were fair; and they took wives for themselves of all that they chose" (NRSV). First Enoch 6:1 records, "In those days, when the children of man had multiplied it happened that there were born unto them handsome and beautiful daughters. And the angels, the children of heaven, saw them and desired them . . ." Later on, Enoch is shown the place that "is the prison house of the angels; they are detained here forever" (1 Enoch 21:10).[5] This appears to be not only the background of Jude 6, but also of 2 Peter 2:4.

Whatever the background of his comment about the fallen angels, the point made by 2 Peter 2:4 is straight forward—not even beings who by nature belong in heaven were spared when they sinned. How much more certain is the punishment awaiting earthly beings who sin?

Peter's second example is taken from the time of Noah. We read about this in Genesis 6:5–8:22. God observed that as humans multiplied in the earth, sin tended to multiply as well; as it says in Genesis 6:5, "Every inclination of the thoughts of their hearts was only evil continually" (NRSV). As a consequence,

1 and 2 Peter

God destroyed everybody, aside from Noah and his immediate family. The consequences of sinful behavior were severe!

2 Peter 2:6-16: Examples of Sodom and Gomorrah and Balaam

Sodom and Gomorrah and the rescue of Lot. In both the Old and New Testaments, Sodom and Gomorrah are a byword for immorality (e.g., Isaiah 1:9, 10; 3:9; 13:19; Jeremiah 49:18; 50:40; Amos 4:11; Matthew 10:15; Romans 9:29). In Genesis 18:16–32, we find Abraham bargaining with the Lord for the lives of those in Sodom. The Lord said that He would spare the city if as few as fifty righteous people were found there. Abraham continued to negotiate until they agreed that if a mere ten righteous people could be found there, then the city would be spared destruction. In the event, not even ten righteous people could be discovered, and only Lot and his family escaped the judgment of God on that city, although at the last minute his wife looked back and was turned into a pillar of salt (Genesis 19:1–26). Second Peter 2:6–10 contrasts the fate of Sodom and Gomorrah with that of Lot. Lot was rescued because he was distressed by the "licentiousness of the lawless" (verse 7, NRSV). This incident also demonstrates that the "Lord knows how to rescue the godly from trial" (verse 9, NRSV).

False teachers and the path of Balaam. Second Peter 2:10–16 launches into a full-out attack on the false teachers. They revel in the daytime (verse 13); they have eyes full of adultery (verse 14); and they entice unsteady souls (verse 14). They have left the straight path[6] by following the path of Balaam son of Bosor (verse 15). Balaam's actions are described in Numbers 22:1–24:25. The elders of Moab and Midian had tried to hire Balaam to curse the tribes of Israel. He initially refused, but was persuaded when offered a larger sum of money. In the end, he could only prophesy what the Lord permitted, and he pronounced three different blessings upon the tribes (Numbers 23:7–11, 18–26; 24:3–9). Peter reacts against Balaam because he is prepared to take money to perform spiritual services that are against the best interests of God's people.

2 Peter 2:17-22: Dangers of turning back to previous sinful lifestyle

Peter is particularly concerned about the fate of those whom the false teachers entice back into their former sins (2 Peter 2:18). The false teachers promise freedom, but as Peter points out, the freedom they promise is different from what Jesus promises. For those that know Jesus, the freedom they have is a freedom from the snares of sin. They have escaped the pollutions and/or defilements of the world (verse 20). By way of contrast, the false teachers also teach freedom. But the freedom they teach is the freedom to behave in a manner that is unconcerned with God's judgment. A freedom, in fact, that allows Christians to behave in much the same way that they had behaved before they became Christians. But Peter describes this as a trap (verse 20). If one behaves in a manner that leads to corruption, then it is not freedom, but enslavement. In fact, for those who had left their pagan lifestyles behind, it is a re-enslavement.

---

1. The table is loosely modeled on that found in Davids, *The Letters of 2 Peter and Jude,* 136–141, who has underlined the words and phrases that he finds in common between the parallels. See also the parallel passages between 2 Peter and Jude (in the Greek text) in Bauckham, *Jude–2 Peter,* 259, 272.

2. So concludes Richard Bauckham, *Jude–2 Peter,* 141–143; Charles Bigg, *Commentary on the Epistles of St. Peter and St. Jude,* 216–224; and Peter Davids, *The Letters of 2 Peter and Jude,* 136–143.

3. Gene L. Green notes, "The literary practice of borrowing thoughts and language from another author was common in the ancient world, even being a foundational practice within the educational system. *Imitatio,* or μίμησις allowed borrowed material to be reworked extensively as it was adapted to an author's purposes," and suggests that "in both language and thought, 2 Peter and Jude run parallel at numerous points, suggesting that we have before us an example of *imitatio.*" In "Second Peter's Use of Jude: *Imitatio* and the Sociology of Early Christianity," in Webb and Watson, *Reading Second Peter With New Eyes,* 2, 7.

4. The word *hell* in the KJV and NRSV versions of 2 Peter 2:4 comes from the verb *tartaroō,* "to hold captive in Tartarus," a verb that is found only here in the New Testament. Tartarus is a place lower than Hades in Greek mythology. The Greek word for Hades, *hadēs,* is the word usually translated as "hell" in the New Testament (e.g., Luke 10:15; 16:23; Acts 2:31; Revelation 1:18; 20:13), although the word *Gehenna* (Greek *geena*) is also translated "hell" on occasion (e.g., Matthew 5:22, 29).

5. The translation from 1 Enoch is that of E. Isaac and found in James

H. Charlesworth, ed., *The Old Testament Pseudepigrapha* (Garden City, NY: Doubleday, 1983), 15, 24.

6. The word *hodos* in verse 15, translated as "path" in the ISV and "road" in the NRSV, has both meanings and can even be translated with the English word *way* ("way" is used as a term for early Christians in Acts 9:2).

CHAPTER 12

"Where Is the Promise of His Coming?"

2 Peter 3:1-18

2 Peter 3:3, 4: False teachers and the delay of the second coming of Jesus

Peter warns that in the last days, scoffers will come (2 Peter 3:4). Indeed, the impression given by Peter's words is that scoffers were already active, and, in his view, their presence is one of the signs of the last days.

The scoffers ask the pointed question, "Where is the promise of his coming?" (verse 4). In doing so, they challenge the long-standing belief of Christians that Jesus will return to this earth, and soon. The scoffers ask how likely that belief is, given that the ancestors have died and "all things continue as they were from the beginning of the creation" (verse 4, KJV). The point they are making is that by the time 2 Peter is written, many of those who had expected the return of Jesus had died without ever seeing that happen. They further argue that if you look back as far as Creation, things have gone on as they have before.

2 Peter 3:5-10: Peter on the timing of the Second Coming

Peter responds to those who deny that Jesus will return in several ways. He first addresses their claim about the unchanging nature of the world. He reminds his listeners that it is *not true* that the world has continued unchanged since Creation. For example, at a time of great wickedness a great change occurred when God destroyed the world with a flood (verse 6). Peter then points to another change that is coming in the future—there will be a great destruction when God again acts against sin, but this time, the destruction will be by fire, not water. Peter insists that the present world is being kept until the day of judgment. God will then cleanse the world with fire (verse 7; cf. Revelation 20:7–15).

Peter then turns to the perspective of God regarding time. He draws on Psalm 90:4, which in the Greek text of the Septuagint would read (in English) something like, "Because a thousand years in your eyes are like the day of yesterday which is gone."[1] Peter states this thought as follows: "With the Lord a day is like a thousand years, and a thousand years are like a day" (2 Peter 3:8, NIV). A short time from the perspective of God may seem a long time from a human perspective. Peter points out that the delay is actually based on the patience of God, who does not want anybody to perish, but that everybody should come to repentance (verse 9).

Peter then points out that when Jesus does return it will be at a time when He is not expected. The day of the Lord will come as a thief (verse 10; cf. a similar saying of Jesus in Matthew 24:43, 44; Luke 12:39, 40; and of Paul in 1 Thessalonians 5:2). The "day of the Lord" is a phrase with a rich Old Testament background, where it stands for a dramatic and destructive future judgment of God (e.g., Isaiah 13:6, 9; Jeremiah 46:10; Ezekiel 30:3; Joel 2:1, 2). Second Peter 3:10 links the day of the Lord to the second coming of Jesus, which will be a time of dramatic judgment in which all evil is consumed by fire.

A thief who comes at night usually expects to sneak away unnoticed. But while the day of the Lord will be as *unexpected* as a thief at night, it will certainly be noticed. As Peter says, "The heavens shall pass away with a great noise, and the elements shall melt with fervent heat" (2 Peter 3:10, KJV). The second coming of Jesus will be unannounced and unexpected, but everyone will know about it when it happens!

2 Peter 3:11-13: What sort of persons ought you to be?

Peter highlights the impact a belief in the soon return of Jesus makes on the everyday life of a Christian. He has a convenient example to draw on of a group of people who have abandoned the belief in the Second Coming—the false teachers and those who influence them. Their behavior reflects that belief. If Jesus will not return a second time and destroy evil, there is no reason to live a moral life. One can live selfishly and sinfully. But "if everything is to be destroyed in this way [at the second coming of Jesus], what kind of people ought you to be? You ought to live holy and godly lives, as you look forward to the day of God and speed its coming" (see verse 11). If one really believes that Jesus will return to punish sin and reward the righteous, then this has profound implications for everyday living (cf. Matthew 24:45–51).

2 Peter 3:14-18: Paul's writings and other scripture

Second Peter 3:15, 16 says some very interesting things about Paul's writings.

First, Peter says that Paul also wrote of the need to live at peace while waiting for the second coming of Jesus and to use the time to develop holy lives. Paul would indeed agree. He says, for example, that God's kindness and forbearance and patience are to lead us to repentance (Romans 2:4; cf. 2 Peter 3:9). Paul might strongly emphasize that righteousness is by faith alone (e.g., Romans 3:21, 22), but he is scandalized if his readers would want to conclude that this gives a license for sin. How, Paul asks, can Christians, who died to sin through baptism, continue to live in it (Romans 6:1–14)?

Second, Peter's reference to the writings of Paul is evidence that Paul's writings were significantly appreciated very early in Christian history. Whether or not Peter is referring to the whole collection of his writings now found in the New Testament or a subset of them cannot be determined. Nevertheless, Peter's comments show that some of Paul's letters had already been collected together by the time he was writing.

Third, Peter comments that Paul's writings can be misconstrued just like other scripture. The Greek word *grapha* literally means "writings," but in this context it clearly means sacred writings, such as the books of Moses and the prophets. Here is very early evidence that Paul's writings had taken on an authority within early Christianity somewhat like the authority of the Hebrew Bible.

Peter warns that it is possible for the unlearned and unstable to twist Paul's meaning to their own destruction (2 Peter 3:16). Earlier, Peter had warned against "false teachers" (2 Peter 2:1–3). In 2 Peter 3:16 we find that they are using Paul's writings to justify their teachings and behavior. The false teachers teach freedom, but the end result is that their followers are snared in corruption (2 Peter 2:13). Their teaching results in licentiousness (verses 2, 3). It appears that the false teachers used what Paul said about liberty and grace as an excuse for sinful behavior. In doing so, they completely misread Paul.

Finally, Peter urges that when Jesus returns, He should find that His church is at peace. Churches are made up of sinful human beings, and so conflicts will inevitably arise. Yet because Jesus gave His life for us and has forgiven us so much, Christians should lead a life of forgiveness and peace.

---

1. Psalm 90:4 corresponds to Psalm 89:4 in the LXX. The translation is that of J. N. D. Kelly, *Epistles of Peter and of Jude*, 360, which renders the idea of the LXX beautifully.

CHAPTER 13

Major Themes of 1 and 2 Peter

Peter addresses very practical issues in his two letters: persecution of the church (1 Peter) and the problem of false teachers (2 Peter). He responds to both these problems with the insights gained through theological reflection. The sufferings of those who are persecuted reflect the suffering of Jesus as He died for our sins. The claims that the false teachers make because Jesus has not yet returned are shown to be worthless in the light of the coming fiery judgment of God. In Peter's theologically informed responses to the issues that he addresses, a number of important themes emerge, several of which will be considered in this chapter.

Eschatology and the biggest story ever told

Eschatology is more than the "doctrine of last things" in 1 and 2 Peter. While we only see glimpses of the complete picture as it is understood by Peter, it is the backstory that explains everything.[1] It is a story with a truly cosmic scale. Peter notes (but does not describe) the creation of the world (1 Peter 4:19) and the fact that Jesus was "foreordained" (KJV) or "destined" (NRSV) before the foundation of the world (1 Peter 1:20). The Christian readers of 1 Peter were also chosen and foreknown or destined (verses 1, 2), and sinners were also "destined" to stumble (1 Peter

2:8). Sin entered the divine realm when the angels sinned (2 Peter 2:4); and sin was so great in the "ancient world" (verse 5) that God destroyed all sinners with a great flood, while preserving Noah and his family (1 Peter 3:20; 2 Peter 2:5). God had a special relationship with His people, the descendants of Abraham and Sarah (1 Peter 3:6). The prophets foresaw, albeit dimly, the coming salvation in the sufferings and glory of Jesus (1 Peter 1:10, 11). In this present time, God has a special relationship with Christians, who are His royal priesthood, His chosen race (1 Peter 2:5, 9, 10). The future will bring judgment of all the living, who will be judged according to their deeds (1 Peter 1:17; 2:23). This judgment will culminate in the fire of God that will destroy all sin (2 Peter 3:10). The final resolution of all things will culminate in the fulfillment of Christian hope, an inheritance kept in heaven (1 Peter 1:3–4).

Eschatology permeates both 1 and 2 Peter.[2] Nowhere are the details of the bigger story set out as a coherent narrative in 1 and 2 Peter, but such a "story" forms the background against which to understand the importance of Jesus in bringing salvation from sin and gives future hope in his second coming. It provides a way that the readers of 1 and 2 Peter can understand their own circumstances and how they should live. They live in difficult times but can understand themselves as participants in a cosmic struggle between the forces of good and evil in the world and live their lives as those who expect to find their behavior scrutinized at the last judgment.

Suffering, Jesus, and salvation

First Peter is written to a group of Christians who suffer sporadic persecution (1 Peter 1:6; 3:13–22; 4:12–19). They live from moment to moment not knowing whether they will be faced with a choice between remaining faithful to their call as Christians and suffering or abandoning their faith to avoid the suffering. Indeed, on some occasions such decisions were life or death decisions, and at any time they had a potential economic and social impact on the lives of Christians. If you were married or if you were a slave, then, within the circle in which you were living, your faith could leave you open to pressure and, in the case of the slave, considerable violence (1 Peter 2:18–21; 3:1–7). Yet Christians undergoing persecution can look to the example of Jesus. He suffered without complaint so that we could have salvation and eternal life. Christians are sprinkled with His blood (1 Peter 1:2), they are ransomed by His blood (verses 18, 19), and by His wounds they are healed (1 Peter 2:22–25). Christ suffered for sins, the righteous for the unrighteous (1 Peter 3:18).

Peter understands Jesus to be a figure of enormous importance. His suffering, death, and resurrection provide a new birth and living hope to believers (1 Peter 1:3), and it has provided them with salvation (verse 5) and an incorruptible inheritance (verse 4). Jesus' second coming will be the day of the Lord and will bring fiery judgment upon all sin (2 Peter 3:10–12). Jesus is not portrayed as an ordinary man in 1 and 2 Peter, but as one of cosmic significance that literally will remake the world in the future, and in the meantime, will provide salvation from sin in the present. Thus the suffering of Jesus had a cosmic consequence. Christians who suffer for their faith also share in the suffering of Jesus, and in their suffering, anticipate the future judgment of God (1 Peter 4:17).

Order in the home, society, and the church

Peter returns to the theme of the regulation of social interactions several times. He speaks both in general and specific terms. In general terms, Christians should be obedient to the authorities, both those of the state (the Roman Empire; 1 Peter 2:13, 14), or the leaders of the Christian community (1 Peter 5:1–5). The officials of the state have a God-given task to punish those who do wrong (1 Peter 2:13, 14), and in so doing, provide the framework for the operation of civil society. Christians, therefore, should be law-abiding citizens, so far as their consciences allow them, given some of the demands that the state made in areas of worship.

Slaves were to submit themselves to their masters (1 Peter 2:18–21) and wives to their husbands (1 Peter 3:1–6). Peter, like Paul (cf. Ephesians 5:22–6:8; Colossians 3:18–24), was no social revolutionary. The freedom brought by Jesus was a freedom from sin (1 Peter 2:24), a freedom to worship God, and a freedom to hope for the future. Christians were to live as free people (verse 16), but this freedom was exercised within the constraints of a well-ordered society and a well-ordered church. Yet as Christianity gained ascendance in society in later centuries, its ideas have provided the impulse for significant social change, while at the same time maintaining a stable society that had the resilience to adapt. The abolition of slavery is but one of many social changes for the better that grew out of impulses founded on Christian understanding.

To other believers, Christians should conduct themselves with respect and mutual love (verse 17). A robust and living faith, after all, would build through goodness, knowledge, self-control, and godliness to its ultimate goal—love (2 Peter 1:3, 4).

Scripture

Most of the writings that make up the New Testament cite the Old Testament as the authoritative word of God. The gospel writers, for example, see the Jesus activities and teachings as fulfillment of Old Testament prophecy (e.g., Matthew 2:15; 4:14; 26:56; 27:9; Luke 4:21; 24:27, 44; John 12:38; 13:18–20; 19:28). Paul also quotes the Old Testament as authoritative (e.g., Romans 3:10–18; 15:9–12; 1 Corinthians 3:19, 20; 6:16; 9:9; 10:7; Galatians 3:6–13). Paul goes so far in 2 Timothy 3:16 to say that Scripture is "useful for teaching, for reproof, for correction, and for training in righteousness" (NRSV).

Peter touches on Scripture and its interpretation in two separate places—both highlighting the centrality of Jesus. In 1 Peter 1:10–12, he points out that the prophets studied their own prophecies to understand the grace that has come to Christians through Jesus. In 2 Peter 3:2, Peter outlines the two places where a Christian can find divine guidance: first through the prophets "of old" (i.e., the Old Testament), then through the words of Jesus as they are given through the apostles.

Finally, Peter notes the special status of Paul's letters (verses 15, 16). They were known in the communities to which

Peter was writing but, like "other scriptures," needed to be studied carefully, lest they be misunderstood (verse 16).

How should we live?

In both 1 and 2 Peter, much attention is devoted to how Christians should live. In 1 Peter, the way Christians live is overshadowed by the potential presence of persecution and suffering. Slaves, for example, will likely suffer for being Christians. But they are urged to do right, because, as Peter asks, "How is it to your credit if you receive a beating for doing wrong and endure it? But if you suffer for doing good and you endure it, this is commendable before God" (1 Peter 2:20, NIV). Other Christians receive similar advice. They are urged to be able to give a reason for their hope, with gentleness and respect (1 Peter 3:15). They should keep a clear conscience, so that when others speak against them maliciously, they will know themselves to be innocent (verse 16). It is better to suffer for doing well than for doing evil (verse 17; cf. 1 Peter 4:15).

In both 1 and 2 Peter, the coming judgment of God acts as a motivation for ethical behavior. First Peter 1:17 states openly that because God the Father will judge all impartially, Christians should live in reverent fear. First Peter 4:7–11 states that "the end of all things is near" (NIV) and lists the consequences of this observation: Christians will be clear minded, self-controlled, and above all, love each other deeply (verses 7, 8).

In 2 Peter, the motivation for holy behavior is highlighted by the contrast that exists between those who deny that Jesus will return and those who live in the expectation that He would return. Those who deny the return of Jesus live lives of dissipation and sin (2 Peter 2:1–3, 17–21), and they have returned to their former lifestyle. As Peter says, "It would have been better for them not to have known the way of righteousness, than to have known it and then to turn their backs on the sacred command that was passed on to them" (verse 21, NIV). By way of contrast, if you believe that Jesus will return to bring fiery judgment to the world, then you will live a holy and godly life (2 Peter 3:10, 11) and will "make every effort to be found spotless, blameless and at peace with him" (verse 14, NIV). The expectation of the soon return of Jesus makes a big practical difference in how Christians live their lives.

In stressing the importance Peter places on ethical behavior, one should not overlook the crucial place that love has in Peter's thinking. Love is the ultimate goal of faith (2 Peter 1:5–7), the basis on which Christians should deal with each other (1 Peter 2:17; 3:8), and the place of love in the life of a Christian is a theme that Peter returns to frequently (e.g., 1 Peter 3:8; 4:8; 2 Peter 1:7).

Ransomed, sanctified, and having genuine mutual love

First and second Peter are short works that come to us from the very earliest days of Christianity and that are authored by one of Jesus' closest confidants who had been a leader in the early Christian movement from its beginnings. They are addressed to the concrete situations of first-century Christians living in Asia Minor, people who are very distant from modern readers in culture, language, and circumstances. Yet as Peter addresses their concerns, he looks at the issues facing these early Christians through a process of theological reflection. In doing so, he provides noteworthy insight into many key areas of Christian theology.

For Peter, the Christians he addresses should be living as those who are ransomed (1 Peter 1:18) and sanctified (verse 2). He urges that they live in mutual love and respect (1 Peter 2:17). They live in difficult times, but can look forward to a glorious hope (1 Peter 1:3). One might sum up the content of his letters as practical advice to Christians living in a time of uncertainty.

---

1. I found M. Eugene Boring's outline of the "narrative" of 1 Peter quite helpful. Boring divides this narrative into "Then" (Creation, Fall, Israel, prophets) and "Now" (Jesus, His death, His sitting on the right hand of God, as the end of history). "Narrative Dynamics in First Peter: The Function of Narrative World," in Webb and Bauman-Martin, *Reading First Peter With New Eyes*, 26–33. I personally would add a third element to 1 Peter's narrative: "Then, Now, Will Be."

2. See, for example, the references to eschatology in 1 Peter that cover two

pages compiled by Robert L. Webb in "Intertexture and Rhetorical Strategy in First Peter's Apocalyptic Discourse: A Study in Sociorhetorical Interpretation," in Webb and Bauman-Martin, *Reading First Peter with New Eyes*, 80–83.

Notes

Notes

Notes

Notes

Notes

Notes

Notes

Notes

Notes